the counseling process

the counseling process

Daniel J. Delaney / Eastern Virginia School of Medicine

Sheldon Eisenberg / Cleveland State University

Rand McNally College Publishing Company
Chicago

RAND McNALLY EDUCATION SERIES
B. Othanel Smith, *Advisory Editor*

Current printing   (last digit)
15   14   13   12   11   10   9   8

To Grace and Marge With Love

Preface

Professionals in counseling seem to spend considerable time arguing over various theoretical approaches to the counseling process. The labels which are used to identify various schools of thought often confuse beginning trainees: behaviorism vs. existential-personal; insight vs. action oriented; neo-analytic vs. eclectic; and so forth. Certain major theorists are identified as belonging to, or are major spokesmen of, one of these camps. By the time the candidate finishes his first basic course in counseling, he is encouraged to identify with a particular theoretical approach and to learn the names of the theorists associated with that approach. This is an especially unfortunate consequence and one which we have tried to avoid by intentionally not parcelling our ideas into one camp as against another.

Because counseling is seen as a process whose purpose is to help clients engage in more rewarding behavior, many of the theoretical arguments, when boiled down, are really philosophical discussions about the nature of man's development. What the various theorists seem to disagree most about, then, is how to label, describe, and explain the processes which accurately account for the growth, development, acquisition, and change of human behavior. Since a counselor exists to help people acquire more rewarding behavior, his intervention strategy is going to be influenced heavily by the concepts and principles he invokes. The basic approach of this book, then, is to develop those principles which appear to have validity in describing human behavior change. We are especially concerned with developing those concepts and principles which counselors may invoke as a basis for determining how to intervene with a given client so as to have the maximum favorable impact in the minimum possible time.

We have tried to integrate the best elements of all the thinking we have been exposed to in developing an approach to counseling. Thus, in Chapter 2 the notions on impact, change, and strategy are heavily influenced by the notions of the systems approach applied to counseling, particularly the contributions of Mager (1962); Ryan (1969); and Thoresen (1969); as well as Kell and Mueller (1966). Our thoughts on congruency and values are heavily influenced by Rogers (1964); Raths, Harmin and Simon (1966); London (1964); and Ellis (1962, 1967). An article by Hobbs (1962) really helped put the role of awareness into greater perspective.

The ideas of those who have emphasized the relationship aspects of counseling have contributed most heavily to our thoughts in Chapters 3 and 4. These include Rogers (1951, 1961, 1964); Carkhuff and Berenson (1967); Truax and Carkhuff (1967). Goldstein's (1962) thinking contributed to our discussion on the relationship between client expectation and counseling process movement.

Some writings which have contributed to our ideas on goal setting in Chapter 5 include: Krumboltz (1965, 1966); Mager (1962); and Mahrer (1968). Many books and articles are available on the basic concepts of testing and the role of assessment and evaluation in the counseling process. Peterson (1968) clearly has had a major impact on our thinking, as does Goldman (1961, 1964).

Chapter 6 is the longest, most comprehensive, and is clearly drawn from a great variety of sources. Bandura's writings helped us develop a basic overview for this chapter (Bandura [1961, 1969]; Bandura and Walters [1963]). Bandura's (1969) book was clearly an effort of monumental proportions. The section on systematic de sensitization was based on the research of Wolpe (1958); Wolpe and Lazarus (1966); and Paul (1966). The reader interested in in vestigating further the notions of training in progressive relaxation may want to explore some of the case studies described in Ullmann and Krasner (1965); and Krumboltz and Thoresen (1969). Hosford (1969) presents a comprehensive review of the research literature in this area, and his review has been followed by some thoughtful commentary.

The counselor's role as an agent of help in making wise deci sions and learning the skills necessary to make wise decisions is emphasized by Krumboltz (1966). Articles by Clark, Gelatt and Levine (1965); Dilley (1965, 1967); Gelatt (1962); and Thoresen and Mehrens (1967) discuss in detail the process by which people make decisions, and the relevance of these notions for the behav ior of counselors. Hamachek (1965) has collected a set of read ings which focus on self-concept development. The ideas of both Hobbs (1962) and Ellis (1962, 1967) contributed heavily to the sec tion of awareness in this chapter. At a broader level, reviews of counseling theories by Patterson (1966), and Ford and Urban (1963) have had a more global impact on this chapter.

Frankly, the contents of Chapter 7 came primarily from our own experiences as counselors. Obviously, a couple of these experi ences were very difficult for our clients as well as ourselves. The notions that we learned and included in this chapter we did not learn easily.

Our intentions in citing these writers are several. First, we wanted to communicate our recognition of and respect for these people for the impact they have had on the development of our ideas. Second, we want the interested reader to be able to pursue in greater detail those ideas which especially interest him. While we obviously value further investigation into the concepts and principles we have developed, as stated earlier, we do not value the reader encapsulating himself into one camp or another. We would much prefer that the counseling trainee keep himself flexible, consider the potential merit of all the ideas he is confronted with, and synthesize these ideas into a theory which will have maximum utility for himself.

1971

DJD
SE

Contents

**Chapter 5.   Goal Identification and Determination
of Counseling Strategies   79**

Chapter 1   Introductory Perspective

People voluntarily seek the help of counselors for many reasons. Some have serious doubts about their worthiness as individuals; they lack a sense of confidence—a sense of self-esteem. Others recognize a difficulty to relate well with significant others. Adolescents with their peers (both in the same and opposite sex), parents with their children, children with their parents, spouses with each other, and employees with their supervisors (and vice versa) are a few good examples. Some individuals experience anxiety to such an extent that it interferes with their ability to function effectively in important situations. Some need help in making important decisions for the future—whether to go to college and which college to go to, which career field to enter into, whether to change jobs, whether to get married or seek a divorce. Some have done things for which they feel guilty, and the intensity of their feelings reaches such strong proportions that they desperately want relief. Some are confused and in turmoil. They no longer know what they believe and do not believe. They need help sorting out their values and beliefs. Some just want to understand themselves better.

Still other individuals do not come voluntarily, but are referred to the counselor by a significant person who is disturbed about some aspect of behavior. The child who talks back to the teacher, the child who never talks in class and never interacts with his peers, the adolescent who constantly gets into fights on the playground, the guy who cannot hold a job for more than two weeks are a few examples.

These are all the people for whom counselors are expected to provide help. The primary purpose of this book, then, is to help students of counseling learn to be effective in working with such people in an individual counseling arrangement. Our objective, therefore, will be to develop those basic concepts and principles which we see as applying to all individual counseling situations. To accomplish this, we will view counseling as a process having a series of stages. In analyzing each stage, we will develop and explore those basic principles which relate to effective counselor functioning during that stage. Certain desirable counselor responses and their potential impact for the client shall also be examined. These basic principles may be seen as applicable in every setting—be it in a counselor's office in a public school, a counseling agency, the client's home, a hospital, or in a private practice.

COUNSELING DEFINED   In the final analysis, the outcome goal of any counseling intervention is to help a person behave in a more rewarding manner. It is the person for whom counseling is intended who determines what is "more rewarding" for him. In this determination the person is aided by the counselor. The assistance that the process is able to offer is determined by the counselor. Whether counseling is or is not psychotherapy is not an important issue to the study of the process. In that the process of counseling is similar to that of psychotherapy, the two terms, "counseling" and "psychotherapy," will be considered synonymously. For the sake of clarity, the counselor and the therapist will be called the "counselor."

Counseling is, therefore, a process by which a person is as-

*sisted to behave in a more rewarding manner. Assistance is deter-
mined by the counselor; that which is more rewarding is determined
by the person being assisted with the aid of the counselor.*

Who Is the Counselor? The counselor is a person who is qualified to offer counseling. The word, "qualification," as used here,
means the successful completion of a graduate studies program,
approved by a recognized professional organization, which includes an experience of counseling practice under supervision.
Such programs usually lead to the certification of the graduate in
a particular area of competency. Examples of these various competencies, under consideration here, are: psychological counseling, elementary or secondary school counseling, pastoral counseling, employment service counseling, vocational counseling,
marriage counseling, and career counseling.

COUNSELING IN A DEMOCRATIC SOCIETY The strength of a
society lies in the ability of its citizens to develop all their talents
to the fullest, to become all that they are capable of becoming, and
to live at their highest level of functioning. In addition, people living in a democratic society have the added duty to help others to
strive for and achieve their self-betterment.

At times, most people find themselves unproductive, inefficient,
unable to function, or find themselves simply unhappy. Most individuals have the capacity to find the needed strength to correct
their difficulties, either by themselves or with the aid of those
close to them. Some persons, however, need the help of those who
possess certain skills in and an objectivity toward solving problems. The counselor is one such professional who can offer assistance to those in need.

The very essence of a democratic social order is that it allows
each citizen to develop his talents, capacities, and abilities to the
fullest. It is no accident, therefore, that counseling as a process
which facilitates individual growth and development is seen as an
integral part of a functioning democracy. This orientation is emphasized especially by counselors functioning in school situations.
These counselors tend to see students in the process of growth,
and see their own role as facilitating that growth process. For

some students, certain environmental circumstances have interfered with their growth and development; they function in what may be described as a "hostile environment." Other students have powerful experiences which interfere with their growth and development. Other students have failed to acquire skills which are basic to functioning in our society. The development of more complex skills depends upon the prior development of these basic skills. Failure to acquire basic skills will have an interfering effect on the student's growth and development.

Developmental counselors in schools thus try to facilitate growth and development in many ways: by helping clients work through traumatic events; by helping them acquire certain basic or more complex skills; by helping them learn to cope more effectively with the hostile aspects of their environment; and by modifying significant aspects of the environment believed to be related to the child's growth and development. The last orientation identifies the counselor as an environmental engineer—a person who works with the environment of the client, rather than the client.

Over the past several years, the number of individuals seeking counseling assistance has increased. Indications of this increase are evidenced by the waiting lists of agencies offering counseling services. Whether the increase is a result of the stress and strain of modern living, the increased availability of agencies offering counseling, a growing positive attitude toward such services, or other variables, the fact is that more people are seeking the aid of counselors. There is a need, therefore, for counselors to offer the most appropriate help possible to the greatest number seeking such assistance. This requires that counselors learn to be of maximum service to their clients in the quickest, most efficient, and effective manner possible.

This orientation to short-term counseling means simply that the assistance offered to one who seeks counseling is no more than what is needed to help this person to live in a more rewarding manner. It is not a "cure" for a problem; it is not "in depth" therapy; nor is it a process for the restructuring of an individual's personality. It is a form of help to bring more happiness to the individual, to permit him to function better, and, in general, to give him a more satisfactory way of life. No specific time limit can be given for the length of the process. However, environmental variables do put limits on the amount of available time. To be considered are such variables as mobility of the population, school vacations, and semester schedules.

FOR WHOM IS COUNSELING INTENDED? The person who avails himself of counseling is called the "client," or "counselee," or "patient." For purposes of clarity the term, "client," will be used. The client is (a) anyone who comes to the counselor for assistance, or (b) anyone who is referred to the counselor by a significant person in the client's life. The client is one who seeks help in correcting some behavior that is unrewarding to him, that is making him unhappy or leaving him unsatisfied, that is not "proper" or "good" as he sees it, that is harmful to him in some manner, or, more simply, that is something he would like to change or which significant others in his life (parents, teachers, spouse, etc.) may want him to change.

COUNSELING AS A PROCESS We have previously described counseling as a "process," and that term conveys much about what counseling is. The term, "process," means a sequence of events which takes place over *time*. The past and the future impinge on the immediate present during any counseling session. Both client and counselor bring to each session the learning experiences of the past. Each brings not only the skills and talents he has learned, but also the beliefs, values, attitudes, and basic assumptions he has acquired from past experience. Counseling, as a time-sequence process, is oriented toward the future. Client and counselor have come together to help the client function more effectively in his future. Thus, both must project the client into the future and ask, "What will help this client most in his future functioning?" Counseling is also a process of the present, for the way the counselor functions with his client here and now indicates what he hopes and believes will make the difference in the future.

Thus, the counselor is a person who must focus on the past, present, and future. He must understand what the client has learned from his past, anticipate what will be in that client's future best interest, and ask himself, "What may I do and how may I act toward this client in the present which will have the most impact with him?"

Counseling as a time-oriented *process* may be differentiated from other human interactional processes by its stages and direction of movement. These stages are applicable regardless of the goals or expectancies of the client. Whether the goal is to help a person to reach some educational objective or decision, some vocational decision, some understanding of the world he has made for himself or was made for him by others, or to attain some general psychological health, the stages of the process remain basically the same.

THE STAGES OF THE PROCESS

Stage 1—The Initial Session The first stage in the counseling process is the first meeting—the interview or session—that point in time where the counselor and the client meet for the first time for the express purpose of the counselor helping the client toward a goal through the counseling process. The criteria for gauging a successful first session will be covered in Chapter 3.

Stage 2—The Facilitative Relationship The second step in the process of counseling is the establishment of a facilitative relationship. This term, "relationship," has been used so often in psychological jargon that if it is not properly and operationally defined it can become a confusing concept. The relationship is an essential stage in the development of the counseling process. It is necessary for two people working together to trust each other. It is necessary that the counselor accept the client; that both are truthful and open in their communication; that both are honest—honest in terms of personal commitments and honest in terms of value orientations and differences. In the establishment of this relationship, within the context of counseling, the one variable the counselor must control is his own behavior. This stage in the development of the relationship will be covered in Chapter 4.

Stage 3—Goal Identification and Determination of Counseling Procedures At some time in the counseling process, the counselor will ask himself, "What help does this client want from me?" "What is it that the client would like to change?" "How can I best help the client to change?" These questions, in addition to others and the answers to these questions as well as the criteria for these answers, will be discussed in Chapter 5.

Stage 4—Counseling Strategies   In the fourth stage, the counselor implements the counseling procedures or strategies in a way that will have maximum impact with the client. Once the counselor knows what the client expects or wants of him and after the counselor has determined how he can best help the client, these procedures are what the counselor follows to help the client move toward his stated objective. The use and evaluation of various counseling strategies by the counselor will be covered in Chapter 6.

Stage 5—Termination and Follow-up   The termination of the counseling process takes place at the point when the client has met his behavioral objective or when the client can do the things he wants to do and be the kind of person he wants to be. There are some problems involved in the termination process. Criteria for the immediate and post-termination period should be applied to produce a successful ending as well as to insure the overall success of the counseling process itself. These criteria, as well as procedures for the follow-up necessary to assess the effectiveness of the counseling itself, will be covered in Chapter 7.

The demonstrational typescripts and case study data used throughout this work are taken from the files of the authors or from the files of their student counseling trainees. In order to understand more fully the description of the process of counseling, it is necessary to come as close to real observational examples as possible. Therefore, following some chapters will be typescripts of interviews and demonstrative observational examples, to aid the reader in more fully understanding the descriptive material presented.

SUMMARY

Counseling is defined as a process in which a client is assisted by a qualified counselor to behave in a more rewarding manner. The client decides, with the aid of the counselor, what help he needs; the counselor decides on the way to help the client.

The qualified counselor is one who has completed an approved program of graduate studies and is professionally certified as a counselor. The client is one who seeks the aid of a counselor, or who is referred to the counselor for assistance.

With the increasing number of persons seeking help, a short-term approach to counseling is necessary, if such services are to reach all who seek help.

Counseling, as a process which takes place over time, may be characterized by its stages of development: Stage 1, the initial session; Stage 2, the establishment and maintenance of the facilitative relationship; Stage 3, the identification of the goal for counseling and the determination of the use of appropriate counseling procedures; Stage 4, the use of counseling strategies; and Stage 5, the termination of the procedures and the follow-up for evaluation of the counseling effectiveness.

SUGGESTIONS FOR
FURTHER READING

Arbuckle, D. S.
    1965 *Counseling: Philosophy, Theory and Practice.* Boston: Allyn and Bacon.

Blocher, D. H.
    1966 *Developmental Counseling.* New York: Ronald Press.

Bordin, E. S.
    1955 *Psychological Counseling.* New York: Appleton-Century-Crofts.

Carkhuff, R. R. and Berenson, B. G.
    1967 *Beyond Counseling and Therapy.* New York: Holt, Rinehart and Winston.

Combs, A. W. and Snygg, D.
    1959 *Individual Behavior.* New York: Harper and Row.

Ford, D. H. and Urbana, H. B.
    1963 *Systems of Psychotherapy: A Comparative Study.* New York: John Wiley.

Hobbs, N.
    1962 "Sources of Gain in Psychotherapy." *American Psychologist,* 17:18–34.

Hosford, R.
    1969 "Behavorial Counseling: A Contemporary Overview." *The Counseling Psychologist,* 4:1–33.

Kell, B. and Burow, J.
    1970 *Developmental Counseling.* New York: Houghton Mifflin.

Kesey, K.
    1962 *One Flew Over the Cuckoo's Nest.* New York: New American Library, Signet.

Mahrer, A.
    1968 *The Goals of Psychotherapy.* New York: Appleton-Century-Crofts.

Pepinsky, H. B. and Pepinsky, Pauline.
    1954 *Counseling Theory and Practice.* New York: Ronald Press.

Phillips, E. L. and Wiener, D. N.
    1966 *Short-Term Psychotherapy and Structured Behavior Change.* New York: McGraw-Hill.

Porter, E. H.
    1950 *Introduction to Therapeutic Counseling.* Boston: Houghton Mifflin.

Shertzer, B. and Stone, S. C.
    1968 *Fundamentals of Counseling.* Boston: Houghton Mifflin.

Truax, C. B. and Carkhuff, R. R.
    1967 *Toward Effective Counseling and Psychotherapy.* Chicago: Aldine Press.

Chapter 2　Principles of Behavior Applied to the Counseling Process

This chapter is devoted to developing some important concepts and principles which transcend all the stages of the counseling process. The first proposition of the book is that all human behavior, including the behavior of the counselor and the client in the counseling situation, is purposive and goal directed. We consider this statement to be true whether or not there is any awareness as to the purposes and goals of one's behavior. The counselor's primary goal is to achieve the outcome goals of counseling his client, and to behave in such ways as to facilitate progress toward the attainment of those outcome goals.

A second proposition is that in order to attain certain important long-term goals, it may be necessary to first attain certain more immediate goals. As the review of the counseling stages suggested, most counselors view the establishment of a relationship of mutual trust, openness, and honesty as one such immediate goal. The counseling process will proceed only after this relationship has been achieved. Attainment of this relationship is necessary and instrumental to the successful attainment of outcome goals. A major task for counselors is to *anticipate* with each client other process goals for this successful attainment of outcome goals.

A third proposition is that associated with any given action or sequence of actions is a variety of consequences. It is important to distinguish these along two dimensions: observable vs. nonobservable consequences and immediate vs. delayed consequences. Thus, four types of consequences can be meaningfully discussed: immediate and observable, immediate and nonobservable, delayed and observable, and delayed and nonobservable.

Suppose in the course of counseling, a counselor says to his client, "Perhaps the reason you turn people off is that you are really afraid of them." The client thinks for a second and says, "You're right! I never thought about that before." Insofar as the counselor is concerned, the client's response was an *immediate and observable* consequence of the counselor's response. Suppose the client also thinks to himself, "Wow, this counselor really understands me thoroughly." Since the counselor could not observe the client thinking that to himself, the client's thought is an *immediate but nonobservable* consequence of his statement.

Suppose further, the client goes home and continues to think about what the counselor had said, and he thinks about it a lot. As far as the counselor is concerned, that client's activity is a *delayed and nonobservable* consequence of his response. Suppose, even further, the client comes in the following week and says, "You know, I did a lot of thinking about what you said to me last week. You really hit the nail on the head. I am afraid of a lot of people, and I realize that I need to work through my fears about other people." This last is clearly a *delayed and observable* consequence of the counselor's response.

Therefore, counseling effectiveness is related to the counselor's ability to accurately *anticipate* the consequences of his actions with his client. Since some consequences are delayed and others are nonobservable, accurately anticipating consequences of one's actions is clearly a difficult task. Nevertheless, the more accurately a counselor can anticipate the impact of his behavior with his client, the more effective he is likely to be with his client. Perhaps one way of defining sensitivity is in the ability to accurately anticipate the impact or consequences a person's behavior has on another person's subsequent behavior.

People tend to behave in ways that their actions will result in consequences which are consistent with their desired goals. It may also be said, then, that effective human functioning is related to the ability to behave in ways which will result in consequences which are consistent with desired goals. To do so requires that people be aware of desired goals and potential consequences. Since certain consequences of any act are delayed and nonobservable, accurately anticipating consequences can be a difficult task.

Often people behave in ways which will result in consequences that are inconsistent with their desired goals. Some are not aware of the discrepancy between goals and consequences. A good example might be the case of the counselor whose process goal is to help the client feel safe, secure, and non-threatened so that he will talk more fully. In the course of the first encounter, the counselor may respond, "I think you're being somewhat selfish about this matter and not very fair to your teacher." The consequence of the counselor's response at this point in the counseling process is likely to be threatening to the client, sufficiently so, that he might not return for another session. Clearly, the counselor's desired goals and actual consequences were highly incongruent.

The statements which apply to human functioning in general clearly apply to the effective functioning of counselors. Not only must counselors clearly describe the goals of their intervention with clients, but they must be able to accurately anticipate the consequences of their actions in the presence of their clients. The counselor's task is to behave so as to make a favorable impact upon his client; that is, an impact which will facilitate and not interfere with the acquisition of counseling goals. To do this, the counselor must be a person who has a clear description of outcome goals, who can accurately anticipate the impact of his actions upon his clients, and who can clearly relate present impact for the attainment of future goals.

Another important dimension involved in the analysis of consequences is that of value judging. Value judgments are basically statements concerning the desirability of certain actions or consequences under certain conditions. Counselors who say that clients should engage in self-examination are making value judgment statements about what is good and desirable for their clients. Thus, consequences are frequently analyzed as to their desirability or preferability. Since counselors are interested in attaining certain consequences with their clients, being able to size up a set of predicted consequences against a set of value statements is an essential counselor skill. He must be able to say, given his values, whether certain consequences, if they were to occur with his client, would be evaluated as favorable or unfavorable, desirable or undesirable.

Suppose a fourteen-year-old girl seeks counseling because she is very confused about a lot of things and generally "up tight." In the course of counseling, she begins to become aware of a feeling of strong anger toward her parents and as a result begins to feel a good deal of guilt about those angry feelings. How is the counselor to view these consequences of his intervention? Should he see what is happening to the client as good and desirable? As bad and undesirable? As an inevitable set of events? Should he deal with these consequences, and if so, how? Clearly, in order to answer these questions, the counselor must come to grips with the value judgments he is making about his client, that is, the statements he is making about what is in the client's best interest. He must also deal with his own feelings should such consequences occur. Might some counselors feel guilty about the influence they may have on the client? Might some feel afraid because they are not sure how to help the client work through his feelings of guilt?

Another example. Suppose a seventeen-year-old male high school junior seeks the counselor's help because he is having difficulty getting along at home as well as in school. He has no friends, his grades are poor, and his life is depressing, boring, and lonely. In the course of counseling, the client decides for himself that the best way to cope with these problems is to quit school and join the military. The counselor happens to know that his parents would be most upset with this decision. Again, what counselor value judgments are involved? Does he assume the boy capable of making wise decisions for himself and thus accepts the decision even if it might incur the wrath of the boy's parents? Does he take the position that finishing high school, no matter how arduous the task, is really in the boy's best interest, and so tries to persuade him to finish? Does the counselor take the value position that people have the right to make their own decisions and that the obligation is to themselves to think through the consequences of their decisions? With this viewpoint, of course, the counselor would want to say to the client, "Well, that is a possible alternative open to you, but before you act on it, I think it might be important to think through the consequences. . . ." "What are some of the things you think might happen if you chose this course of action?" Once the client has looked at the consequences, the counselor might follow up by saying, "What are some of your feelings about whether those consequences would be good for you or not?" The purpose of this last counselor goal-directed response, of course, would be to help the client clarify for himself some of the value judgments he is making for himself about the consequences of his actions.

There are times when the goals a client wants and desires are goals the counselor values as not in the client's best interest. Such a condition is considered a value conflict situation. A good example would be the counselor who values client self-exploration and self-examination while working with a client who does not value these things for himself. Counselor and client are in a value conflict situation. They disagree as to what is good and desirable for the client. *Counseling cannot succeed when a value conflict exists between client and counselor as to what is in the client's best interest.* If counseling is to be successful, such value conflicts must be eliminated. This means that someone's values must, of necessity, be changed. Thus, the effective counselor must be aware of the value judgments he is making as to what is in the client's best interest, aware of the discrepancies that exist between himself and his client; and he must be prepared to resolve such discrepancies.

If thinking through the goals of one's actions, the potential consequences of these actions and the value judgments associated with these actions and consequences is part of what counselors must do to help clients, then this is also part of what a counselor can do to help a client do for himself. Implementing this process was demonstrated in the case of the seventeen-year-old male previously discussed. It will be explored in more detail in Chapter 6 (Counseling Strategies) in the discussion of the decision-making process.

BELIEFS, VALUES, ATTITUDES, AND ACTIONS Any discussion of the counseling process must consider the interrelated notions of values, beliefs, attitudes, and philosophical assumptions. These factors are stressed especially in the client-centered theory of counseling. Within that model are some important concepts related to the role of values in the counseling process. The primary focus of this discussion will be on the relationship between values, beliefs, attitudes, and actions, and with what client-centered writers describe as "congruence." When using this concept, they seem to be referring to the notion of internal consistency among one's beliefs, attitudes, and values. In the use of this term, it is clearly communicated that they believe it is desirable and good that all elements and components of one's belief system should be internally consistent with all other elements and components of one's belief system. Further, it is desirable that one act in ways which are consistent with one's belief system and to avoid acting in ways which are inconsistent with one's belief system. One may really understand value orientation of this position by contrasting it with a position espoused by Ralph Waldo Emerson when he said, "Consistency is the hobgoblin of little minds."

Some important constructs in the counseling literature may be described using this basic model. Enhancing, facilitating, or contributing to a client's growth and development is generally seen as an important counseling goal. Few people, if any, ever achieve complete congruence in the sense described. It may not be possible to ever achieve a state of complete internal consistency among all the important elements of human functioning. And yet, perhaps, one way to conceptualize growth and development is to see it as a process over time of continually assessing and reappraising one's beliefs, values, attitudes, and actions and continually modifying these components in the direction of greater congruence. Change in the direction of greater congruence or internal consistency may be seen as growth. The process of "self-actualizing" may be seen as the process of coming closer and closer to a state of congruence between self-as-is and self-as-would-like-to-be. If this model is viable, it suggests that service to some clients is to help them become more aware of their values, attitudes, beliefs, and underlying assumptions, aware of the discrepancies among these components, and aware of what changes will result in greater congruity. It must be pointed out that such an approach might be more appropriate for a bright, introspective person interested in greater self-understanding, and less appropriate for a resistant, defensive client. It is also an approach which may be more appropriately implemented at a later, rather than an earlier stage of counseling. Premature implementation of this sort of approach may be especially frightening to some people.

Another concept very much related to this basic model is "genuineness." Genuineness is generally described as an essential characteristic of a counselor that is directly related to his effectiveness. The concept has been used often by a variety of writers with a variety of meanings. Sometimes it seems to mean "honesty," other times, "candid self-disclosure." Perhaps one operational description of genuineness is *being aware of one's values and beliefs, and when one acts, to always act consistently, never inconsistently, with those beliefs, values, and attitudes.*

Using this description of the concept, developing into a genuine person is a process that requires *awareness.* Clearly, becoming aware of one's beliefs, values, and attitudes is a necessary and instrumental part of the process of becoming a genuine individual. With emotionally stable, introspective, and nondefensive people of adolescent age, or older, sensitivity groups are frequently used as an approach to facilitate the growth and awareness process. Counselor education programs frequently require a sensitivity group experience for their students precisely on these grounds. Their rationale is that genuineness is an important characteristic of counselors, that becoming aware of one's beliefs, values, attitudes, and underlying assumptions will contribute to the enhancement of this quality, and that a sensitivity group experience is a powerful approach to achieve those self-learning goals. It should be noted that such groups do have a powerful impact on their members, and that with some people, the impact is intense and negative. That is, for some people these groups may be threatening and may interfere severely with their growth and development. For a few, the experience may have a downright destructive impact.

In discussing the belief systems of counselors, it is also generally held that if counselors are to be effective they must hold certain values and beliefs and act consistently with those values and beliefs. Thus to be effective, it is held that the counselor must value honesty. He must believe that the client has an inherent right to be treated with respect. (An interesting question: A counselor expresses anger toward a client for something the client did or said. Is the counselor communicating respect for the client?) The counselor must believe that the client has the capacity for favorable change. The list of "desirable counselor values" is inexhaustible. Rather than list them all, we encourage the reader to think through the desired value positions he believes he must hold and act consistently with them to be effective.

To help you get started, we suggest you envision yourself working with each of the two clients presented earlier in this chapter. For each client ask yourself two basic questions, "With this client is it good and desirable that . . . ?" and "Is it good and desirable that this client . . . ?"

What many people discover as they go through this process is that there has been a limitless number of values they have been acting consistently with, without awareness. A value judgment the authors of this book are making is: It is good and desirable for counselors to be aware of the value statements they make as to what is in the best interest of their clients.

AWARENESS   A major strategy of almost all traditional face-to-face counseling intervention systems has been to facilitate some kind of client "awareness." The various systems have differed with regard to what they want their clients to become aware of, but all have agreed that a major way to help clients function more effectively is to help them become "aware of" something. Their underlying operating assumption is that a causal relationship occurs between gaining awareness and improvement of functioning. Thus, client improvement would occur if, and only if, the client was to gain awareness. If clients do not change, it is because they have not gained sufficient awareness. If they do change, it is because they have gained insight.

The assumption of this functional connection between awareness and change has been seriously challenged, especially with the development of the operant conditioning approach, a system which does not assume awareness and defines what is learned as associations between a stimulus and a response.

Part of the challenge has been based on scientific grounds. Many clients considered to have demonstrated awareness did not demonstrate change, and many who demonstrated change did not demonstrate awareness. A second challenge stems from the question, "awareness of what?" Where each system has differed has been in the kind of things counselors have wanted their clients to become aware of. Thus, psychoanalysts have wanted clients to become aware of certain alleged underlying motives that the therapist assumed to exist, whereas rational emotive therapy has held as an essential awareness-based process goal where the client becomes aware of certain illogical self-feeding statements he is making which disrupts his functioning.

Clearly, the kinds of things the counselor hopes to help his client become aware of would have a great deal to do with whether or not counseling change could be facilitated. It is one thing to work toward change by trying to facilitate awareness of alleged unconscious processes; it is another thing to try to help a client change undesirable behavior by helping him become aware of the consequences of his undesirable behavior. In each case, the counseling approach of the counselor would differ considerably. For instance, if a counselor decided that an essential process goal would help make his client aware of certain unconscious processes, his treatment would be different, say, from treatment he would use if he saw awareness of consequences as an essential process goal for his client.

Thus, facilitating certain kinds of awareness may be seen as a valuable process goal for certain clients with certain difficulties, whereas, for other clients with other difficulties facilitating awareness is not an instrumental process goal. Facilitating awareness of underlying values is also a desired process goal for some clients, particularly clients who are bright and do not resist the examination of values. As will be developed shortly, awareness of dominant emotions and the situations in which they occur is yet another valuable awareness-based process goal. For clients whose counseling goal is to make important life decisions (career, future education, etc.), becoming aware of the skills that are necessary for effective future performance and of interests that will be necessary for the enjoyment of future positions are essential process goals. It is also essential that clients become aware of their behavioral characteristics which are related to their decision. Consider the case of a young man who must decide whether he wants to sell insurance or do computer programming but who demonstrates social withdrawal. His behavioral characteristic in this instance would interfere more with his ability to function as an insurance salesman than as a computer programmer.

Thus, what the counselor chooses to base any part of his intervention approach on facilitating client awareness will depend on the goals of intervention and the characteristics of the client. He is much more likely to implement an awareness-based approach with a non-defensive, highly motivated, bright, self-referred client whose concern is related to a value conflict than with a defensive client (referred by another), who demonstrates little motivation and whose concern is high-test anxiety. The particular kinds of things the counselor wants his client to become aware of are also related to client behavioral characteristics and counseling goals. For a client whose social behavior is aversive to other people, awareness of social consequences of his interpersonal actions may be an especially valuable process goal, whereas awareness of values may have limited relevance. For a client caught in a religious dilemma, but who gets along well with others, just the opposite may hold true. Chapter 6 discusses effective counselor strategies for facilitating awareness.

EMOTIONS AND THE COUNSELING PROCESS   Helping clients understand and work through powerful emotional experiences has generally been considered an essential aspect of the counseling process. Empathy may be described as the counselor's ability to understand how his client feels at any given point in the counseling process and how he may feel about the situations he is describing to the counselor. Empathy also refers to the ability of the counselor to respond to the client so as to communicate that the nature and intensity of the emotion experienced is understood by the counselor. Thus, counselors who have some functional understanding of human emotions are more likely to be empathic and impactful than others who do not.

Much about human emotions, especially "unhappy" or "negative" emotions, may be understood as an extension of the basic principle that human behavior is purposive and goal directed. "Frustration" is a key concept in understanding much about human emotions. Frustration may be defined as a situation in which a person has an important goal or set of goals that he is unable to attain. In some situations, significant factors of the environment serve to block the attainment of important goals. To a person driving a car, getting home may be an important goal and encountering a series of red traffic lights may represent a series of frustrating situations. In this example, significant aspects of the environment created the frustrating situation.

In other situations, frustration may occur because the person does not have the necessary or appropriate behaviors in his repertoire to attain his goals. Suppose a person comes to a counselor and says he just does not seem to be able to get along well with others and that he finds it difficult to establish and maintain friendship relations he very much wants to. Upon discussion, it becomes apparent to the counselor that his client has not learned to respond effectively in social situations and that his inappropriate social behavior "turns people off." He has as a goal establishing and maintaining friendships, but he has not acquired the appropriate behaviors to attain his goal. A relevant counseling goal for this client in this sort of frustrating situation then may well be to help him learn new and more appropriate social behaviors.

What emotional impact does the experience of frustrating situations have on people? Anger, anxiety, and depression may all be seen as basic emotional responses which occur when people have goals they are unable to attain. Under the same frustrating situation different people may react with different kinds of emotions and with different degrees of intensity. Some drivers at red lights react with mild annoyance; others with violent anger. In a classroom test, given the same difficult question, some students will react with mild tensing while others will react with intense anxiety.

The intensity of the emotional response seems partly related to the importance and immediacy of the goal to be attained. To the driver returning home as usual after work, a red traffic light may evoke only small annoyance. But for the same driver who has received a call from his wife that their child has suddenly become ill, that same red traffic light may evoke a more intense anger. Missing an item on a "pop quiz" may evoke mild self-directed annoyance. For the same student (a senior going to college), missing an item on the ACT exams may evoke intensive anxiety.

Thus, emotions may be characterized along two important dimensions: kind (or quality) and intensity. It is meaningful to distinguish among four types of basic human emotions: anger, depression, guilt, and joy. The first three are "negative," or undesirable emotions, while the fourth is a "positive," or desirable emotion, to experience. The first three types of emotions seem to occur as a consequence of frustrating situations.

Associated with these basic emotions are different intensities. Anger may vary from very mild annoyance to violent rage; fear from slight tension to intense anxiety; depression from slight sadness to severe depression. The more frustrating the situation, the more intense will be the feelings associated with the situation.

Thus, if the situation a client is describing can legitimately be identified as frustrating, the counselor may reasonably speculate that the client is experiencing some important feelings associated with that situation. By responding not only to the emotion but to its apparent intensity, the counselor is communicating real empathy to the client.

If certain emotions occur as a consequence of encountering certain frustrating situations, then a way to help clients deal with their emotions is to help them deal effectively with the frustrating situation. The most adaptive way to deal with frustrating situations is to operate on the environment in such a way as to remove the obstacles to goal attainment. The involved counselor may help in several ways. One way is by helping the client identify the obstacles to goal attainment and by then identifying socially acceptable ways they can be removed. A second way is to help the client learn more effective ways of dealing or coping with situations. For example, for the client who has not learned effective social skills, learning these skills would help him more effectively attain his goals.

It is not always possible to remove obstacles to goal attainment. Under some conditions, the best a counselor can do is be empathic with his client, understand his feelings and help him learn to tolerate the difficult situation. Counselors in schools face this situation regularly. Students frequently complain about a particular teacher. The counselor may believe that the criticism and hostility are justifiable and may find himself agreeing that little can be done to change the teacher's obnoxious behavior. The best he can do is let the student communicate his feelings freely and help him find more effective ways to cope with the situation.

"Hope" is an important concept in human functioning. Hope usually refers to an individual's expectation concerning the likelihood that he will attain his goals. When he sees no chance at all, he is said to have given up hope. People under these conditions are likely to experience depression. The more valued the goal, the more severe or intense the depression. For the depressed individual, a relevant process goal in the treatment stage of counseling (after an optimal relationship has been established) may be to work with the client to help him find hope. Once this goal has been attained, the chances of alleviating depression are enhanced for many clients.

Anxiety, fear, nervousness, and tension all seem to describe the same kind of emotion which comes under several broad types of situations: when a person's safety and security are threatened; when he sees himself not capable of adequate or competent performance (either by his own or someone else's standards of competency); and when his sense of self-worth and self-esteem are jeopardized. Some people seem to experience uncontrollable anxiety which appears closely associated with a specified set of situations. Examples might include: uncontrollable test anxiety; debilitating fear of public speaking situations; debilitating fear of situations where one is being evaluated by a significant other, such as a parent, teacher or friend; fear of riding in airplanes. The only control a person has over his anxiety in these situations appears to completely avoid the situation which elicits the anxiety. For people experiencing such difficulties, systematic desensitization appears from current research literature to be a treatment approach of high potential. This approach is described in detail in Chapter 6.

Other people seem to experience broad and diffuse anxiety across a whole variety of seemingly unrelated situations. One also senses from such people, a feeling of self-doubt and insecurity. Helping such people acquire a more favorable sense of self-worth and a greater sense of personal security would seem important process goals, which if achieved, would lead to reduced anxiety. This notion is considered in more detail in the section on self-concept in Chapter 6.

Guilt is an extremely important human emotion that may be understood by the "congruency" concept described earlier. Thus, guilt may be seen as an emotional response occurring when a person evaluates himself as having behaved in ways which violate a significant moral or ethical code. The more valued the code that was broken, the more severe the guilt. Frequently, the violation involves some other person, and in violating the code, the client has done harm to the other person.

In the presence of clients experiencing and reporting guilt, many counselors tend to try to persuade the client out of his guilt. People do not like to hear others say bad things about themselves. A typical counselor response to a person experiencing guilt might be: "You shouldn't feel guilty because. . . ." Such an approach by the counselor is very unlikely to have its intended impact. The harder the counselor tries to persuade, the more resistant clients are to being persuaded. Further, the counselor must assess his own values and ask himself how he would feel under similar circumstances. Clearly, it would be highly ungenuine to try to persuade a client not to feel guilty if the counselor himself were to feel guilt under the same circumstances.

People experiencing guilt frequently have as a goal a need to atone for their sinful act. Capitalizing on this desire to atone may lead to a more viable counselor approach. The search between client and counselor for the appropriate act of atonement would constitute an approach which, in the long run, may have a high and favorable impact for the client. Since the guilt usually involves another party, the act of atonement would also, of necessity, involve that other party. In order to implement this strategy, the counselor must not evaluate the client's guilt, but rather accept it non-judgmentally. Further, the client, not the counselor, must be the one who decides what constitutes an acceptable act of atonement. The counselor can serve as a facilitator in helping the client evaluate the situation, but the counselor cannot make the judgment for the client.

Thus, it seems clear from this section that a counselor must be a person who is capable of understanding and responding to his client's feelings, especially in the early sessions of counseling. Invoking the principles discussed above will help a counselor more accurately anticipate, and, therefore, more accurately respond to the feelings his client is experiencing. The basic principles also anticipate some potential treatment approaches for clients who are experiencing negative emotions.

IMPLICATIONS FOR COUNSELOR EFFECTIVENESS Imbedded within these principles are some immediate implications for a counselor to enhance his effectiveness. If the counselor's behavior is purposive and goal directed, then obtaining a clear description of the particular goals of counseling for each client is an important factor which will enhance his effectiveness. A counselor's effectiveness is also directly related to his ability to identify those process goals which must be attained to reach these outcome goals.

"Creativity" is frequently defined as the ability to make a variety of responses to specified situations, or sometimes the ability to generate a variety of alternatives to deal with important situations. A counselor's effectiveness is directly related to his creative ability; that is, his ability to generate a variety of approaches for reaching favorable impact with each specific client. Perhaps one of the real goals of counselor training programs relates to helping trainees become more creative—to generate new and different counseling approaches.

Yet another way to enhance counselor effectiveness is to help counselors more accurately anticipate the impact or effects of the counseling approaches open to them. Given that some important consequences are delayed and nonobservable, this can be a difficult skill to attain. Yet part of the training counselors go through to be effective involves helping them to learn to anticipate delayed and unseen consequences.

If the beliefs and values that people hold are said to influence their behavior, a way to help counselors function more effectively is to help them become aware of their beliefs and values and aware of what it means to act consistently with those beliefs and values. In parallel fashion, if feelings and emotions influence the way people function, then helping counselors become aware of their feelings and the social interactions in which those feelings occur will also enhance their effectiveness.

Clearly, the emphasis is on the behavior of the counselor in the counseling process. The quest is to work toward finding answers to this question: What kind of counselor approaches will have what kind of impact on what kind of client having what kind of concern at what stage in the counseling process? The question may be turned around: What may a counselor offer to a particular client so as to have maximum favorable impact with the client at any particular point in the counseling process? Also, given a variety of counselor approaches available to a counselor at a particular point in the counseling process with a particular client, what sort of impact will each of these approaches have with the client? Which set of impacts will be most favorable or desirable at the present time and in the future of the counseling process?

The material in the following chapters will work toward clarification of these questions, and will work toward answers to them.

SUGGESTIONS FOR
FURTHER READING

Almond, R., Keniston, K. and Boltax, S.
1969 Patient Value Change in Milieu Therapy. *Archives of General Psychiatry*, 20:339–351.

Arbuckle, D. S.
1965 *Counseling: Philosophy, Theory and Practice.* Boston: Allyn and Bacon.

Bandura, A.
1961 "Psychotherapy as a Learning Process." *Psychological Bulletin*, 58:143–159.

Buhler, C. B.
1965 "Aiding the Patient to Find His Identity and the Values Consonant with It." *Psychotherapy*, 2:89–91.

Combs, A. W. and Snygg, D.
1959 *Individual Behavior.* New York: Harper and Row.

Curran, C. A.
1968 *Counseling and Psychotherapy: The Pursuit of Values.* New York: Sheed and Ward.

Ellis, A.
1962 *Reason and Emotion in Psychotherapy.* New York: Lyle Stuart.

1967 "Goals of Psychotherapy." In A. H. Mahrer, ed. *The Goals of Psychotherapy.* New York: Appleton-Century-Crofts.

Goldstein, A. P.
1962 *Therapist-Patient Expectancies in Psychotherapy.* New York: Pergamon Press.

Hobbs, N.
1962 "Sources of Gain in Psychotherapy." *American Psychologist*, 17:18–34.

Kell, B. and Burow, J.
1970 *Developmental Counseling.* New York: Houghton Mifflin.

Kell, B. L. and Mueller, W. J.
1966 *Impact and Change: A Study of Counseling Relationships.* New York: Appleton-Century-Crofts.

Krasner, L.
1962 "Behavior Control and Social Responsibility." *American Psychologist*, 17:199–204.

1962 "The Therapist as a Social Reinforcement Machine." In H. H. Strupp and L. Luborsky, eds. *Research in Psychotherapy*, vol. 2. Washington, D.C.: American Psychological Association.

Krumboltz, J. D.
1965 "Behavioral Counseling: Rationale and Research." *Personnel and Guidance Journal*, 44:383–387.

1966 "Behavioral Goals for Counseling." *Journal of Counseling Psychology*, 13:153–159.

Krumboltz, J. D. and Thoresen, C. E., eds.
  1969   *Behavioral Counseling.* New York: Holt, Rinehart and Winston.

London, P.
  1964   *The Modes and Morals of Psychotherapy.* New York: Holt, Rinehart and Winston.

Mager, R. F.
  1962   *Preparing Instructional Objectives.* Palo Alto, Calif.: Fearon Press

Peterson, D. L.
  1968   *The Clinical Study of Social Behavior.* New York. Appleton-Century-Crofts.

Raths, L., Harmin, M. and Simon, S.
  1966   *Values and Teaching.* Columbus, Ohio: C. E. Merrill.

Rogers, C. R.
  1964   "Toward a Modern Approach to Values: The Valuing Process in the Mature Person." *Journal of Abnormal and Social Psychology,* 68:160–167.

Ryan, T. A.
  1969   "Systems Techniques for Programs of Counseling and Counselor Education." *Educational Technology,* 9:7–17.

Thoresen, C. E.
  1969   "The Systems Approach and Counselor Education: Basic Features and Implications." *Counselor Education and Supervision,* 9:3–17.

Chapter 3   The Initial Session

The initial session in the counseling process represents the first time the counselor and client meet for the purpose of counseling. Both may have met and spoken together prior to this for the purpose of testing, test interpretation, information giving-seeking, an intake interview, and so forth; however, these meetings are not to be considered part of the initial session. The initial session expresses the first meeting in the formal counseling process.

The client comes to the counselor seeking assistance. The counselor is an individual who is trained to offer such assistance. The setting is an office or small room. After introductions are exchanged, and both are seated, the counselor's responsibility is to help the client talk. Such initiating counselor response leads as, "How may I help you?" "What would you like to talk about?" are in order. Whether the client comes voluntarily, that is, "on his own" or whether he has been sent, or referred, by someone else, the initial session basically proceeds in this manner. The exception is that if the client has been referred, and the referral agent has communicated with the counselor concerning the client, the counselor should make this known to the client, stating what he knows, in general terms, about the client, and then proceed with an appropriate initiating response lead.

THE GOAL OF THE INITIAL SESSION   The counselor has two primary objectives during this meeting: (1) to create an atmosphere in which the client can feel safe to say the things he wants to say, and (2) to help the client realize that the counselor is listening, and understanding what the client is saying.

A number of variables or factors which clearly emerge in the initial session have a great deal to do with whether counseling will be a valuable experience for the client. These variables have a major impact on the later stages of the counseling process. Some of these factors may be viewed as client-related, while others may be seen as counselor-related.

IMPORTANT CLIENT VARIABLES   The client's expectations, attitudes, and behaviors about such things as the nature of counseling, who the counselor is, what things should and should not be discussed, whether counseling will or will not be of help, will have a persuasive influence on the present and future of the counseling process. Some client-held expectations will facilitate the counseling process; other expectations and attitudes will have a severely interfering effect. Where the client's expectations interfere, they must be brought into the open by the counselor and dealt with candidly. Optimally, a client would enter the initial session with the following expectations: that he will have to talk openly and candidly about what is bothering him, even if it is embarrassing; that he will have to work at least as hard as the counselor to understand himself and the factors that are related to his problem; that he is an active participant in the process; that it is safe to talk about things, even if they are threatening; that counseling is a process of self-examination and introspection; that the counselor is a competent source of help; that the counselor is not there to work the client's problems out but to work with the client to help him work out his own problems; and that this may take more than a couple of meetings to do.

Optimally, from the very beginning of the initial session, the client would demonstrate the following behavioral tendencies: introspection and self-examination; complete candor and honesty (nondefensiveness); awareness of feelings, beliefs, and values; quickness to understand the counselor's responses; and the ability to translate new awareness into action.

Clients having optimal expectations and tendencies can be characterized as bright, articulate, self-reflective, and socially poised and accepted. Unfortunately, few clients are of such progeny. Many clients enter the initial session with various combinations of diametrically opposite expectations and tendencies. Thus, a client might enter expecting that he will not have to do much talking or introspecting, that the responsibility for help lies solely with the counselor, that the counselor will change things for the client, that the client will be a passive recipient of the counselor's curative attempts, that the counselor may not be trusted, and that the counseling situation is not safe.

Consistent with these expectations, counselors are likely to see some of the following behavioral tendencies in the client: the tendency to be silent, and when the client does talk, to be resistant and defensive; the tendency to avoid introspection; the tendency to lie, deceive, mislead, and imply by innuendo; the inability to be aware of feelings or gain awareness from counselor's remarks; the inability to translate what is being discussed into new ways of functioning and coping; and the tendency to blame others for his own difficulties. Clearly, where the client's expectations and entering behaviors are of the sort which may interfere with counseling, an important process goal will be one that will influence the client so that the necessary changes can occur. Counseling will not proceed very far if the client continues to maintain such interfering expectations and behavioral tendencies.

Some of the less than optimal expectations and tendencies are worth pursuing in greater depth. Clients frequently enter the initial session with the expectation that the counselor is going to "cure" them. They see the intervention of the counselor the same way they see medical intervention. They go to be "fixed" and the professional's responsibility is to do the fixing: "The expert will wave his magic wand and I'll be cured." This client orientation has a significantly disruptive effect on the counseling process, for by adopting this orientation the client absolves himself of any responsibility for involvement in the helping process. While this orientation may or may not be appropriate in medical intervention, it is emphatically inappropriate in effective counseling. The counseling process proceeds best if all parties involved are actively involved and accept responsibility for their involvement. This same client orientation also suggests an unhealthy dependency relationship. To a degree, the mere fact that clients come seeking the help of a counselor casts the counseling relationship into a dependency mold. However, it is one thing to say that the client's improvement depends upon the skillful intervention of the counselor; it is quite another thing to say that the client is a passive, sponge-like recipient of the counselor's intervention procedures.

Other clients enter with the expectation they are going to be analyzed. Their minds are going to be picked clean by this voyeuristic counselor. He, therefore, represents a threat, and engaging in counseling becomes a threatening situation. A related expectation held by clients who have certain aspects of their life they consider embarrassing is that the counselor will find out about those secrets. While it is probably true that the client and counselor will discuss confidential material, whether that is awful or not depends upon how the counselor handles the situation.

Another client expectation that significantly disrupts the counseling process is the expectation of punishment. This is especially true of clients who have been other-referred and who have had a history of getting into trouble. Their expectation is that the counselor is going to punish them for these inappropriate and trouble-making behaviors. In schools, for example, a teacher privately tells the counselor of a student who he thinks needs the counselor's help. The counselor subsequently sends a note and pass to see the student at a designated time and place. At best, the student has no idea why the counselor sent for him. He is confused and in a state of ambiguity. More likely, his expectation is that he is to be punished for something. Clearly, the client's confusion and inappropriate expectations will have an important effect on both the initial and subsequent counseling sessions.

There are many reasons why clients seek the help of counselors on their own. Some clients are hurting desperately. Their situations are terrible and they are at the point where they can no longer cope effectively without someone's help. Other clients come in for help in making important decisions: career, future education, or marriage. They need someone to help them think through the factors related to their decision. Still other clients come voluntarily to the counselor because they recognize they are neither coping effectively with their environment nor functioning effectively in it.

Some clients are self-referred; other clients are referred to the counselor. Sometimes these referred students come willingly; at other times, they come reluctantly and clearly under duress. Whether a client is coming on his own or is referred by another person has a great deal to do with what happens in counseling; however, the process itself is the same in both situations.

IMPORTANT COUNSELOR VARIABLES During the initial session and throughout the counseling process, the counselor has but one vehicle at his control, one set of variables which he can manipulate: himself and his own behavior. The counselor's task is to help the client, but he can do nothing for the client unless the client is willing and aware of what the counselor is doing. This willingness of the client is the result of the counselor's interaction with him, and this interaction can be controlled only by the counselor as regards his own behavior. This variable of the counselor's behavior includes his verbal (vocal) and nonverbal (nonvocal) communications.

RELATIONSHIP BETWEEN COUNSELOR'S BEHAVIOR AND THE GOALS OF THE INITIAL SESSION To the extent that the counselor behaves in a manner conducive to creating an atmosphere which allows the client to express himself, will the client express himself. Also, to the extent that the counselor behaves in a manner in which his listening and understanding is the focus, will the client come to believe that the counselor is listening to him and attempting to understand him. In other words, the attainment of the goals of this session is directly influenced by the way the counselor behaves. Facilitative counselor behaviors and their impact with the client may be characterized as follows: relaxation, which will help to establish a relaxed atmosphere; listening, from which the client learns that he is the focus of attention; understanding, from which the client learns that what he is saying is important; patience, from which the client becomes aware that he can "pace" himself and need not hurry nor say things about himself or his environment that he may not be ready to say; and motivating the client to return for counseling.

Relaxation   It is important that a relaxed atmosphere be created in this session. A counselor can work toward this goal by using himself as a model for the client to emulate. The counselor should be comfortable and relaxed in the same manner as he would normally relax in a social-personal interaction and setting. A male counselor may serve as an effective role model by doing such things as removing his jacket, loosening his tie, and taking a comfortable posture in his chair. The particular methods of modeling relaxation will, of course, take various forms depending on the personality of the counselor, what he feels comfortable doing, whether the counselor is a man or a woman, and whether the client is a boy or girl, man or woman. Basically, if the counselor models a state of comfort and relaxation, this should help the client learn to be comfortable and relaxed in the counseling setting, and in time, the relaxed atmosphere will be established.

Listening   Listening is a behavior that does not come easily to most people. One can hear, but not listen. Listening implies an attempt to perceive the vocal and nonvocal communications of another, and an attempt to demonstrate this perception. The counselor cannot ask questions and listen at the same time, for while the client is answering, the counselor will be formulating the next question in his mind. Questions such as, "How old is the client?" "Where does the client live?" "Is the client single or married?" "In what grade in school is the client?" only lead to irrelevant and immaterial answers which only become important if the client feels they are important. If the client believes these data are important, in the proper atmosphere and with the counselor listening, he will provide such information.

Counselor questions, or counselor probing response leads, damage the client's perception of counseling. By listening, the counselor demonstrates to the client, and thereby teaches him, that the success of counseling is dependent upon the client's acceptance of his responsibility to communicate to the counselor who is willing and intent upon listening.

Understanding   It is essential that the counselor demonstrates that he understands what the client tells him. The counselor must listen attentively and consciously attempt to be aware of what the client is saying, the implications of the client's remarks for his well-being, and the meaning the client attaches to what he is saying. Appropriate counselor responses at this time may be, "I understand"; "I realize what you are saying"; "I understand what this means to you." On the other hand, if the counselor is having difficulty understanding, he might express himself as, "I am having some difficulty understanding what you are saying; could *you* help *me*?" Understanding can only be achieved by paying attention. Therefore, the counselor must give the client his undivided attention, must be intent upon listening to what the client is saying, and attempt to understand what he is saying.

Patience   The client has come to the counselor for a purpose. It is not the counselor's task to "draw out" this purpose from the client. Rather, the counselor must allow the client to come to a point where he states the help he is seeking on his own and in his own time and in his own manner of expression. The counselor does not necessarily have to accept the first purpose from the client, depending, of course, on the gravity of the problem. Many clients present a problem which is not accurate, either because they do not know what counseling is, or they are not sure of themselves. By being patient, the counselor can help the client to examine his own goals and objectives of counseling and allow him to pace himself in stating these.

Motivating   If the counselor behaves in the manner described, the client will realize he is being listened to, that the counselor is attempting to understand him, that the counselor is giving him the opportunity to speak at his own rate and in his own time. This should provide the client with the proper motivation to continue in the process. Also, the setting is relaxed and comfortable; for most clients this is sufficient for their motivation. For some, however, the need for assured help is greater. If this is stated by the client ("Can you help me?"), or understood by the counselor, the counselor should offer some need satisfaction. Usually a statement such as, "I believe that we can work this out" or "I believe I can help you" is appropriate.

COUNSELOR REFLECTIVE RESPONSE LEADS (CRRLs)   It has been emphasized that the behavior of the counselor is purposive and goal directed. Certain counselor responses are intended to have certain kinds of impact with clients. Some counselor responses are intended to help orient the client's thinking and subsequent responses in certain directions—to look at a particular aspect of what he has said more deeply and intensely, and perhaps from a different angle. The counselor reflective response lead is a particular type of counselor response which, if used judiciously, accomplishes a number of these goals. This sort of response may affect the client in the following ways. First, if the CRRL is feeling oriented, the response will help the client reach and identify his own feelings. This is usually considered an important process goal of counseling, especially those forms of counseling which are oriented toward greater self-understanding. Second, such counselor responses will help a client think in greater depth and detail about the issue he is discussing. Third, in order to make CRRL effective, the counselor must listen carefully. Therefore, by using an effective CRRL, the counselor is communicating that he is listening closely, that he is tuning in, and at that moment in time, the client is his sole concern.

Thus, the CRRL may be used to *reflect* content (what was said by the client), or feeling (what was experienced as a feeling by the client while he was speaking). The reflective lead is simply a "mirroring back" to the client.

Example A

Client: I have trouble with my reading comprehen-
           sion. I have to read something three or
           four times before I pick it up, and I don't
           feel my study habits are too good. [*With
           stressed voice*] I'm flunking out.

Counselor: [*With feeling*] The possibility of flunking
           out has got you really worried.

Client: Oh, lemme tell you, has it ever! In fact I'm
           really *scared* about it. . . . [*Pause*] [Cer-
           tain nonverbal cues of client clearly sug-
           gest that he is thinking this through to
           himself] In fact so scared that I get to
           thinking about it while I'm reading and
           that makes my reading comprehension
           even worse! What a vicious circle!

Example B

Client: My father died last month and since then
           life has been miserable. My mother has
           really taken it hard. She cries an awful
           lot and she's very depressed. I want to
           help her but I don't know what to do.

Counselor: You want very much to help your mother
           but you just simply don't know how you
           can be of help.

Client: Yes, that's absolutely right! And if you were
           to see how badly she's taking it you'd
           really realize how desperate I am. I'm
           afraid she might do something drastic.

In Example A, the counselor chose to reflect a *feeling* that the
client communicated, while in Example B, the counselor chose to
select and reflect a particular *theme* of the client's statement. In
both cases, the impact of the response was to help the client develop his thoughts more fully and in greater depth. In Example A,
the client was helped to communicate the full force of his feelings.
The counselor's response helped him to communicate more openly

and with less inhibition. In Example B, the counselor might have chosen to respond instead by saying, "Seeing your mother so depressed has really upset you." This might very well have led the client to respond with something like, "Yes, you're right. My father's death was a pretty bad blow to me. It was tough enough to have to cope with that! But having to cope with my mother, too, is more than I can take. I feel like I'm falling apart!"

This analysis of Example B has demonstrated that at certain points in the counseling dialogue what the counselor says to the client will significantly influence the direction, content, and nature of future dialogue. Points at which the counselor's response will have such a significant influence may be described as critical incidents or critical situations. At such points, no matter what the counselor says, his response will influence the direction of future dialogue. Two important counselor skills which are involved in this critical incident notion are: first, the ability to identify such critical situations when they occur; and second, the ability to *anticipate* the direction in which the counselor wants the dialogue to proceed. To a degree, any counseling incident may be considered a critical situation. However, certain of these critical situations will have a greater impact on future direction than other situations may have. In a sense, certain interchanges may be considered more critical than other interchanges. It is essential to recognize that a counselor's effectiveness is directly related to his ability to accurately identify the critical situations, and to anticipate which of the possible directions will have maximum value for the future progress of the counseling process.

Imbedded in this notion is the concept of *timing* or *pacing*. Involved in the counselor's decision as to which direction to take the counseling process at these early critical situations is his assessment as to whether the client is ready and emotionally prepared to proceed in that direction. This is especially important in orienting the dialogue toward the client's feelings. Especially during the initial interview, some clients are prepared to fully examine their feelings while others are unwilling to do so. For other clients, certain topic areas are taboo. They might strongly resist discussing a particular dimension of their functioning. Some clients refuse to discuss their homes; other clients will refuse to discuss a particularly acute embarrassing incident, and so forth. If during certain critical situations, the counselor tries to influence the client to discuss these difficult areas before the client is prepared to do so, the counseling process is likely to become threatening. The client is likely to become even more resistant and defensive, and is likely to quickly terminate counseling. If the counselor believes that discussing a particular taboo area is necessary and instrumental to successful counseling, he will first have to prepare (or help the client to prepare himself) to discuss this taboo area. Preparing the client to discuss these areas may thus be seen as an important process goal of counseling.

More will be discussed about critical incidents and deciding on which of several possible directions is valuable for proceeding in later chapters. It is worth saying at this point that part of a counselor's effectiveness is related to his ability to function in the present with his client so as to prepare himself for a more powerful impact in future sessions. By proceeding carefully in the first few sessions, in the long run, the counselor may allow himself to have greater favorable impact upon his client.

If timed well and used judiciously during the initial session, CRRL may have a strong and favorable impact upon the client, and upon the counseling relationship. However, some counselors use it excessively. Excessive use of this response lead will eventually have an extremely irritating effect with many clients. They begin to show anger and annoyance toward the counselor and this usually has a disruptive effect on the relationship.

THE REFERRED CLIENT   One very important factor which influences a client's expectations is whether he has come voluntarily or whether he has been referred by someone else. Clients referred by others frequently represent certain difficulties in the initial session, which self-referred and self-motivated clients do not. The sources of difficulty lie in the entering expectations and behaviors of the other-referred client, and because of these factors, special counseling strategies are sometimes required to deal with these clients. Such clients are frequently confused as to why they are seeing a counselor. They frequently do not feel a need for change, are more likely to be hostile, withdrawn, and/or resistant, and are frequently silent.

They speak when spoken to, answer questions as little as possible, and initiate nothing voluntarily.

Dealing with such clients is especially difficult. The essence of counseling is open communication, and counseling cannot proceed very far if communication is not attained. Counselors frequently try to cope with this situation by asking questions: "How old are you?" "Where do you live?" "How many brothers and sisters have you?" It should be pointed out that the purpose of this question-asking strategy is generally to establish communication. Actually, obtaining the information is only of minor importance. The difficulty with the question-asking strategy is that it generally fails to obtain its intended consequence. Rather, the net impact is that the two people involved fall into a trap. The counselor falls into the role of interrogator and the client becomes the answerer of questions, but he initiates nothing.

Thus, more effective counseling strategies must be found to cope with the other-referred and/or silent client. One strategy is that of candid honesty about how and why the client was "summoned": "One of your teachers noticed you seemed to be unusually withdrawn lately, was concerned about this, and thought it might be worthwhile if you and I could talk about it." For many clients, the net impact is favorable. The counselor communicates that he and the client are there to be task oriented, to talk about the client, and that the counselor is there to be of service. Further, by communicating openly and candidly (straight-from-the-shoulder), the counselor is communicating that he expects the same from the client. His response also allows the client the option of disagreeing with what the teacher observed. This is important, for it is too easy for this sort of confrontation to sound accusatory.

THE CRITERIA FOR ASSESSING A SUCCESSFUL INITIAL SESSION In order for the counselor to assess his success in an initial session, the following criteria are offered, in question form:

1. How comfortable was I during this session?
2. How comfortable did the client seem?
3. Was I relaxed or at least model a relaxed state?
4. Did the client appear relaxed?
5. Did I consciously try to listen attentively?

6. Did the client realize by his behavior that I was listening?
7. Did I understand what the client was saying and did I tell him so?
8. Did the client realize by my behavior that I did understand him?
9. If I did not understand what the client was saying, did I ask *him* to help *me?*
10. Did the client help me to understand him?
11. Did I allow the client to pace himself and avoid use of the probing response leads?
12. Did the client perceive he was responsible to talk and not feel under pressure "to get to the point"?
13. Was the client motivated for counseling and, if not, did I satisfy this client's need?
14. In brief, did I behave in a manner which was conducive to creating a relaxed and comfortable environment in which the client felt free to express himself?

Acting consistently with these principles is not always easy. Many counselors communicate expectancies and biases to the client and then attempt to look for support for these expectancies. If these expectancies are inaccurate, a serious strain in the relationship occurs. The client has come to the counselor for help and assistance. It is up to the client, in his own time and manner, to determine how he wants this help, in what area he seeks assistance, and why he desires it. The counselor must control those expectations he would like to project onto the client, and to listen to, and to understand what the client is saying.

The focus of this session is that the client, with the help of the counselor, through his behavior and the atmosphere he has created, will communicate to the counselor those relevant things about him and the world in which he lives, and those things which the client feels the counselor should understand about him in order to help him.

If a client is to gain from his experience with the counselor, he must feel free to talk openly and candidly with the counselor. Especially, he must feel completely free to talk about the things concerning himself which bother or disturb him the most—things which might cause him embarrassment if he were to disclose them to someone other than his counselor. When most clients first come to counseling, they are not sure how free they can be with a counselor. Therefore, in the initial stages of counseling, to avoid embarrassment and feelings of pain, many clients will avoid talking about the very things which disturb them. Instead, they will talk about things which are relatively safe—things which will not be embarrassing or upsetting to talk about.

Thus, in the early stages, the counselor may well have the vital task of helping the client feel free and relaxed so that he can talk about these disturbing things. Several ways the counselor can facilitate the client's relaxation and thus reduce his inhibitions are listed below:

1. The client will feel more relaxed if the counselor appears to him to be relaxed. The counselor can communicate that he is relaxed by:
   a. The tone of his voice.
   b. His rate of speech.
   c. The fluency of his speech.
   d. His posture.
   e. His facial features, especially eyes and mouth.
   f. The focus of his gaze.
2. The counselor can also facilitate the client's state of comfort by listening and paying attention, by letting the client talk at his own pace without interruption and by communicating that he is trying to understand as fully as possible.
3. The counselor can further facilitate client relaxation in the early stages of counseling by avoiding a question-asking orientation, by not imposing any evaluation on the client or his behavior, and by not demanding that the client clarify confusing aspects of his discussion. Such clarification may be important, but in the initial stages it is more important to help the client relax so that he can talk freely about himself and the things that bother him. The consequences of demanding clarification, at this time in the process, may inhibit the client from discussing what may be the important things to him (and, therefore, to the counselor).

If the client feels comfortable and safe with the counselor, then he is more likely to return for a second visit (and maybe a third and fourth) than if he feels threatened. The point of making the client feel comfortable, relaxed, and safe cannot be overemphasized. These conditions are absolutely necessary if the client is to gain anything from his encounters with the counselor. The counselor can do much to facilitate these conditions; if he is not careful, the counselor can also do much to interfere with the attainment of these necessary conditions. *If the counselor is not careful, he can do much to create the diametric opposite of these necessary conditions.* The counselor and the client cannot possibly succeed if the client does not return.

CASE OF PAUL   Paul W. was a thirty-five-year-old noncommissioned officer. He had requested vocational counseling and had taken a battery of tests. This is his first session of counseling. The process of self-exploration is clearly demonstrated in this interaction.

From Client 6 and after, the client is assessing and evaluating his talents as well as activities of most and least preference. Probably the most significant choice point situation is at Client 1, where the counselor chose to facilitate open-ended self-exploration rather than to provide immediately test information as the client requested at Client 1.

The counselor's rationale, as he communicated at Counselor 2, was that self-exploration would provide a context within which the test information would be more meaningful. Having first looked at and evaluated himself he would be better able to accept and understand the conclusions he could validly draw about himself from the test information.

Counselor:	What can I do to help you?
Client 1:	Uh, you should have a folder on me over here.
Counselor 1:	Um hm. I have it, but . . . can you tell me a little bit more about why you wanted to take tests, and. . . .
Client 2:	Yah. I'm getting out of the service in, uh, five years and four months, and I'm taking courses right now, college

courses, and I don't want to take just anything haphazard, you know, hit and miss. I wanta find out more what my interest lies in and, uh, like if it was electronics, I would wanta take courses to help me toward the electronics degree, or find out what courses to take that's going to help me once I retire from the service. This is primarily all I was interested in . . . something that my interest is, what I'd do best in. I don't know, I don't think any of those tests I took was an IQ test. I don't know.

Counselor 2: Um. Maybe, um, you know, when these tests are interpreted, they're interpreted in the light of what you like to do and what you've done and this type of thing. They'd be a lot more meaningful to me if you could tell me more about yourself. Do you understand what I mean?

Client 3: Um hm.

Counselor 3: The tests, they're kind of meaningless just by themselves. They have to be fitted into a picture of you. I think they're much more helpful to you, too. You know, you think of them in terms of many things about yourself.

Client 4: OK. What would you like to know?

Counselor 4: Just tell me a little bit about yourself, and . . . anything you think is relevant to that whole area, and I think a lot of things are.

Client 5: Um, something like a life history or something?

Counselor 5: Whatever you think is important. You know the choice of a vocation takes in all kinds of areas—of, um, what you like to do, and what you don't like to do, and what you've done before.

Client 6:   Well, I've done a lot of things. Uh. When I was sixteen years old I left home and went to work in the oil fields, and I bummed around the country—slept in a few jails here and there. Then I came back and finished high school. And I never, oh, I never did do much sports—never played that much. I'd go out for them, for a while, until I'd get tired of them and quit. And then it was either come in the service, come in the Air Force, or get drafted, and uh, I came in the Air Force, and uh, while I've been in the Air Force I've held several jobs. I flew for seven years—on flying status, traveled all over the world. I've been in all different countries. I like to go to different countries, do things that they do in their countries—go native, I guess you'd call it—run around with the local populace. I have more or less *pushed* myself towards electronics, because I've always been told this is the field to get into. Uh, I went to, when I was first in the service, I went to radio maintenance school, fixing radios, but this was down in St. Louis and Mississippi, and myself and some of my friends, we liked to drink and carouse around, so I got kicked out of school there, so I didn't, I just wasn't really interested in it. And, when I got grounded from flying status, then I did start going towards the electronics career field. And since then, well, I've put in a lot of self-study—correspondence courses in electronics. I don't like it, don't like really to study, but I did—not, not as well as I should have, I know that. Ah, let's see. Uh, I am an umpire; I referee ball games—baseball, football. I don't particularly like *it* either, but I do it.

Counselor 6:   You don't like it?

Client 7:   No, 'cause everyone's always fussing at me. You can't make any right decisions. And what, what really gets me is when they say something to me, I can't say something back to them. This is the main thing. I don't mind doing it, but I just don't like to take what they have to say to me.

Counselor 7:   It's kind of frustrating, huh?

Client 8:   Um hm. Uh. I took up band for a while, or started out in band—dropped that right fast. And I always wanted to play the guitar. This was strictly self-study there also. I never did finish it either because it just seemed like a waste of time, more than anything else.

Counselor 8:   Um hm.

Client 9:   Uh, yes, when I got grounded, when they kicked me off flying status, I started in with physical conditioning—running, exercising, things like this. This is what I like—I like anything that has to do with physical conditioning, and I took up judo—got up to a brown belt in that. And, fact is, I'm going down today and run a couple of miles. I like to get out and exercise. I like physical work. If I have to do work, I like to do physical labor. And, as I indicated on one sheet I filled out, that I would just like to deliver mail—just be a postman, really. Or operate a gymnasium, something like that. Something that doesn't require a great amount of mental ability. That might help me a little bit. But, uh, I'm actually afraid to try to do anything because of the wife and kids. I don't want to strike out on something so that they wouldn't have security, in case I got killed, or something like that. O.K., so I have to push myself towards electronics, or something like that, that has a good retirement plan, once I start out in a new career. And that's about it.

Counselor 9: I see, you're limited by retirement. The field you go into has to have a good retirement.

Client 10: Um hm. Ya. It has to have *security*. I don't want to just get started and work a couple years, then get fired or something like this; I want to go into something that has some security to it.

Counselor 10: I see.

Client 11: And the post office field is the one I selected because you do get to walk around. Just like these civilian jobs here on the base—they can't fire you, just about—Civil Service. And that's why I go toward the Civil Service career field, because even if you don't work, well, they keep you on the payroll, and they won't fire you. So that's the main reason I want Civil Service.

Counselor 11: Uh hum.

Client 12:   And that's about it.

Counselor 12:   Um, you said *mainly* you'd like to do exercising. So, is the post office job—that's a possibility for you.

Client 13:   Um hm. Ya, well, just because you get to walk around, and it doesn't take any great amount of mental strain to read the name on the letter and drop it in the mailbox, see.

Counselor 13:   But, uh, what you'd really like to do is not good in terms of security for your family, is that it?

Client 14:   Um, is to do what?

Counselor 14:   The judo and exercising, the teaching of that.

Client 15:   Oh, if I did that, that would mean that I wouldn't have any job security, or anything. I'd probably do that just, just as I could, part-time, you know. I need a job with security, is what I need, when I get out of the Air Force.

Counselor 15:   What are you doing now, Paul?

Client 16:   I'm teaching right now—the automatic flight control systems. It's the system that flies the aircraft, so the pilot don't have to touch the aircraft. These controls fly the aircraft, and that's what I teach. I don't particularly like to teach either.

Counselor 16:   You don't like that.

Client 17:   No, 'cause it's indoors.

Counselor 17:   I see. Is that one of the most important things for you, to be outside?

Client 18:   Not really. Uh, I need to get out every once in a while though.

Counselor 18:   Um hm—as part of your job?

Client 19:   Um hm. I'd like to be able to have a job

where I could do about half and half, I guess, inside and outside.

Counselor 19: Um hm. Um, can you tell me any more about the things that you've . . . what things you have enjoyed doing, and what you haven't, what you don't like to do, or, uh . . . what things you think will be, you know, important to you, when you get out and look for a job.

Client 20: Well, I don't know. . . . Well, when I get out I don't plan on how I, what I want to do is, uh, work with TV a little bit in my spare time, see, work in a post office and do the electronics in my spare time . . . something that I'm not making my livelihood from it, but I haven't divorced myself from it completely.

Counselor 20: Have you, have you worked with electronics before, at all?

Client 21: Just for the last, well, since 1964, when I got grounded from flying. And I plan on taking up golf. . . . That's about all I guess.

Counselor 21: You can't think of anything else to tell me that would be helpful in thinking about a job?

Client 22: Well, the only thing I left out is I just like to drink and have a good time and have parties, but other than that, that's it.

SUGGESTIONS FOR
FURTHER READING

Bingham, W., Moore, V. and Gustard, J.
  1959 *How to Interview.* New York: Harper and Row.

Fear, R. A.
  1958 *The Evaluation Interview.* New York: McGraw-Hill.

Goldstein, A. P.
  1962 *Therapist-Patient Expectancies in Psychotherapy.* New York: Pergamon Press.

Knight, G. F.
  1966 "Skills for the Sometimes Interviewer." *Personnel Journal* (May) 45.

Maier, N.
  1963 *The Appraisal Interview: Objectives, Methods and Skills.* New York: John Wiley.

Rogers, C. R.
  1964 "Toward a Modern Approach to Values: The Valuing Process in the Mature Person." *Journal of Abnormal and Social Psychology,* 68:160–167.

Steinkamp, J.
  1966 "Some Characteristics of Effective Interviewers." *Journal of Applied Psychology* (December) 50:487–492.

Chapter 4 The Facilitative Relationship

In the face-to-face counseling situation described here, a primary task of the counselor is to establish and maintain an optimal counseling relationship. That task is the essence of the second stage of the counseling process. Using the constructs developed in Chapter 2, establishing and maintaining an optimally facilitative relationship is a process goal which must be attained if the later outcome goals are to be reached. Establishing an optimal relationship is an immediate goal which is instrumental to the attainment of long-range goals. Establishing such a relationship, then, is purposive and goal-directed behavior.

There is much written describing the dimensions of various relationships: parent to child, husband to wife, physician to patient, friend to friend, teacher to student, supervisor to employee, and so forth. Many of these relationships have been assessed in accordance with the dimensions most often associated with the relationship. The main variable attributed to someone who relates well to others is usually that he is a "good guy," or a "nice person." Likewise, the manner in which a counselor should relate to a client is capable of assessment and may be described in the same terms as other relationships.

The components of the facilitative relationship (or "good guyness") include the feelings and perceptions the counselor has for the client, the client's awareness of these, and the client's feelings and perceptions of the counselor. The characteristics of these feelings and perceptions are:

Counselor Toward Client	Client Toward Counselor
Empathic understanding	Awareness that the counselor knows how I feel.
Warmth and acceptance	Awareness that the counselor has respect for me, is kind, and accepts me for what I am. The counselor is not harsh or threatening.
Genuineness and honesty	Awareness that the counselor is not a "phoney," nor pretending a facade, but that he is the person he represents to me.
Professional competency	Awareness that the counselor is a person capable of helping me with my problems.

Only when the client becomes aware of the counselor-related characteristics will he feel free and comfortable to say the things he wants to say and at the rate and in the manner he wants to say them. Whether or not the client becomes aware of these characteristics depends upon whether or not the counselor communicates them. In short, the client's impressions of the counselor are directly related to the behavior of the counselor.

EMPATHIC UNDERSTANDING   To have empathic understanding is to *know* how another feels and what he is experiencing without feeling the same way himself. The counselor must attentively try to realize what the client is saying about himself and his world. Given what the client is currently communicating, the counselor must be aware of the potential implications of these notions for the client's future functioning. To be empathic means to be able to infer accurately about a client's feelings, attitudes, and beliefs (which are not frequently observable), from what he is saying (which is observable).

The counselor must attempt to place himself in the position of the client, in respect to decision making, unhappiness, frustration, environmental pressures, in order to understand the client and what he is saying. However, at the same time, the counselor must remember that he is not the client and these pressures are not his, but his client's.

It is not sufficient for the counselor to be aware of feelings, beliefs, values, and future implications. He must also *communicate* these observations, inferences, and awarenesses. When a fourteen-year-old girl comes to the counselor, and after some hesitation, slowly and in a faltering manner with her head bowed and her hands fidgeting, says her parents are about to be divorced, it is not sufficient for the counselor to be aware that the girl is feeling anxious and depressed about the situation with a sense of loneliness, rejection, and abandonment. He must respond to her in such a way as to communicate these awarenesses. With such a client, a counselor response such as, "I sense that this is quite frightening to you and perhaps also that you feel as though your parents do not care for you and have betrayed you" would be highly facilitative at this stage of the counseling process. A counselor could not possibly make such a response if he did not understand the client. Making such a response, then, could not help but communicate to the client an uncommonly sensitive understanding on the part of the counselor.

The impact of this counselor response (CRRL) with this client cannot help but be powerful and favorable. Suddenly, someone has appeared in her environment and has communicated that he can understand her when she tries to express her deepest, strongest, and most private feelings. The sensitivity of this person identifies him as a competent source of help. Once that is done, learning follows, as how to effectively cope with this realistically difficult situation.

Thus empathy as a counselor characteristic requires two basic and interrelated abilities. First, the counselor must identify, recognize, and become aware of certain important feelings, attitudes, beliefs, and values which underlie what the client is saying; this is the sensitivity dimension. Second, the counselor must communicate to the client that he has become aware of and has understood not only the overt but the covert aspects of what the client has said.

Probably the most difficult part of the entire process is the sensitivity dimension—being able to understand the feelings of the client, the events he is talking about, and the relevance of the events to his total life situation and his present and future functioning.

Tuning into certain cues can help counselors recognize and become sensitive to the feelings the client is experiencing. It is the client's behavior, both verbal and nonverbal, which provides the cues which can help him understand the client's feelings.

Words are used to communicate feelings. Thus the counselor can tune into his client's feelings by listening carefully for the words the client uses to describe his feelings and the intensity of his experiences. Certain words or phrases are "red flag" signals. They are descriptions or labels for emotions. When a client uses such words to describe himself as angry, depressed, nervous, guilty, he is clearly describing his emotions. The sensitive counselor is one who listens for these words and when he hears them responds so as to indicate he has understood the emotions they have communicated.

A deceptively simple sensitivity training exercise is to generate a list of words and phrases which are descriptions of feelings. Try this individually, first, and then get together with others who have also done it and compare the lists. See if the emotion-describing words others have thought of help you to think of additional emotions you missed on the first trial. As you compare, see if certain kinds or clusters of emotions emerge from the list; that is, that more than one word describes the same kind of feeling—"nervous," "tense," for example. Also analyze whether certain pairs of words describe the same kind of emotion but in different degrees of intensity as, "irritated," "enraged," for example.

Voice tones are another source of cues which communicate feelings. The voice of a person experiencing anger will frequently be loud, shouting, whereas a person feeling depressed may often speak in soft, subdued, almost inaudible, tones. When people feel anxious, their speech frequently becomes markedly "dis-fluent" —stuttering, repeating words, failing to completely develop sentences, using the expression "uh" excessively.

Certain motor cues are especially important for counselors to observe. The expression of the face, the focus of the eyes, hand movements, the amount of squirming in the chair are all valuable cues from which a counselor may more fully understand his client's feelings. People feeling depressed will frequently keep their heads bowed and their gaze fixated at a spot on the floor. People feeling anxious and tense will frequently wring their hands and squirm excessively in their chairs.

Finally, counselors frequently base their sensitivity on logical inference. Given the situation, the client is describing how might he logically be expected to feel? Even when no other sources of cues communicate it, when an adolescent male tells the counselor that last week he moved out because his father got drunk again, we can expect this boy to feel frightened, lonely, rejected, and bitter. The rare person would be one who would not feel these ways.

This brief description is meant only as a guideline. Clearly, clients who experience the same intensity of the same emotion do not use the same words to describe their feelings. Their voice tones and motor behaviors may be considerably different. Some people, for example, lower their voices when angry, rather than shout; others sit silently with lips pressed tightly together and eyes burning. Further, some clients provide discrepant cues, as in the case of a client who was observed to be shouting, pounding, and kicking the desk. When the counselor responded by saying, "You are clearly very angry about all this," the client responded by saying, "No, just a little irritated is all." Rather than communicating ambiguity, such discrepancies should be seen as indicating something significant about the client.

In the case of the young man whose father drinks, the denial of what seemed obvious to the counselor suggested that the client could not yet accept the identification of himself as a person who becomes angry. The counselor hypothesized from this that the client may feel guilty about experiencing anger, especially anger toward his parents (guilty because he sees himself violating the important moral code, "Honor thy father and thy mother"). In later stages of the counseling process, the hunch was verified and led to significant interaction.

WARMTH AND ACCEPTANCE   The counselor must be a warm and accepting person, one who is sensitive to the feelings of the client, compassionate and kind. Counselors communicate this quality not only through their response leads, but by their voice tones and nonverbal cues, particularly facial expressions. It is essential that the counselor communicate to the client, "I accept you. I see you as a worthwhile person. Even if I disagree with some important ideas you have, I still respect you."

Clearly, the counselor cannot communicate this if he does not genuinely feel that way toward his client. The point is crucial. Every counselor is confronted with clients whose ideas he cannot accept, whose values are so discrepant from his that the counselor finds he simply cannot remain tolerant, and whom he finds impossible to respect. Thus, it is essential that the counselor be aware of these feelings and attitudes toward the client. Where his feelings are incongruent and incompatible with the communication of acceptance and warmth, he must either examine and work through his feelings or refer the client to someone else.

It is important to say, too, that there should be no shame attached when a counselor encounters a client he cannot accept, respect, and treat with warmth. However, when the counselor finds himself being non-acceptant of people in general, he must reassess himself and reappraise his values.

It is important to differentiate between rejection of a person and disagreement with some of his ideas. The two are not synonymous concepts. One can disagree with the ideas of another and still respect him as a worthwhile person. Rejection is the opposite of acceptance, whereas disagreement is simply the act of taking a different position on a debatable issue. Whether disagreement is taken by the client as rejection depends upon the intent with which the disagreement is presented, the voice tone and nonverbal cues in which the disagreement is communicated, and the way in which the communication is perceived by the client. If the counselor does intend to communicate rejection, then it is more likely that the client will interpret the statement of disagreement as a statement of rejection.

In thinking through the matter of communicating acceptance, many trainees ask whether it is appropriate in the early stages of the counseling process to communicate disagreement with certain important notions the client has expressed. The rationale underlying their question is that "being genuine with a client includes being honest with him when I, as the counselor, disagree with an idea of the client. If I fail to communicate disagreement when it occurs, am I really being honest with him? And what does my failure to communicate disagreement represent about my attitudes and feelings toward the client and my relationship with him?"

The answer to this dilemma seems to be whether both client and counselor can differentiate between disagreement with an idea and rejection of another as a person. If both parties can be clear and agree about this distinction, then expressing disagreement, while at the same time communicating respect, is quite possible. In contrast, if one or more parties cannot clearly make this distinction then the distinction must be learned before disagreement can be expressed in a facilitative manner. It is worth noting, too, that for clients who have difficulty making this differentiation it is a valuable growth facilitating experience to help them learn the distinction. In a later counseling process, some counselors will pick up on an area of disagreement, confront the client with the disagreement, and continue by saying, "Here is a place where you and I disagree. What about that? Is that O.K. or is that bad?" Once this interaction has occurred, the counselor can easily help the client to understand that disagreement and rejection are not synonymous. He and the client can then investigate the possibility that the client has been erroneously making this equation in other situations as well.

An especially important point in this relationship building stage is that if the counselor chooses to express disagreement he must do so in a non-threatening manner. If the client becomes threatened and begins to feel insecure and unsafe, his statements will become guarded, cautious, and hesitant. His ideas will not be freely expressed and he may become inhibited about expressing certain important ideas. Clearly, such an oppressive situation is antithetical to having the kind of impact which counselors consider favorable and facilitative.

GENUINENESS AND HONESTY A major portion of Chapter 2 was devoted to the meaning of these concepts and their relationship to values and beliefs. Given these definitions, it is not always easy for a counselor to be completely genuine and honest with his clients. In order to do so, he must first be honest with himself. He must be aware of his own values and beliefs in the counseling situation. And yet, the extent of a counselor's impact upon his client is directly related to his ability and willingness to be frankly candid with him.

Trainees frequently object to this notion. Generally, their objections are centered around the notion, "Aren't there times when being really honest with a client will have a disastrous impact upon him?" Possibly the most disastrous impact a counselor could have upon a client is for the client to discover that the counselor has been ungenuine and dishonest with him. When that happens, whatever favorable impact the counselor may have had previously is destroyed. Given a client who has learned never to trust another, what impact can occur when he decides to take the risk of trusting the counselor and later discovers that taking the risk was a mistake because that counselor was not honest with him? In such situations, where a counselor predicts that his honesty would have immediate negative consequences, he is probably in a better position to be honest, allow the negative consequences to occur, and deal with these consequences, rather than to try to avoid the consequences by being less than candid.

PROFESSIONAL COMPETENCY The client comes to the counselor for help. It is essential that the client realize that the counselor is a trained individual capable of offering help and assistance. The key concept here is *hope*. Frequently, the difference between whether clients change or not as a result of counseling is whether or not they are hopeful that the counselor has the competency to help them.

Some clients seem to need special assurance. If the counselor senses that such assurance is necessary, or if the client asks for it, the counselor is free to offer such responses as, "I believe I can help you," or "I believe that we can work on that problem together," or even, "I find it necessary to get to know you better, and then, I will be able to help you."

Clearly, the kind of interaction which occurs in an effectively functioning counseling relationship is something that rarely, if ever, occurs anywhere else in the client's life. The content of the client's communications is of a personal and private nature. What the client talks about in counseling is not what he usually talks about outside of counseling. If the counselor is working effectively with the client, he is communicating the kind of empathic understanding that no one in the client's past experiences has ever communicated before. Perhaps the essence of the counselor's impact is precisely his ability to behave differently, and in so doing, communicate a different set of beliefs toward the client more than anyone the client has previously encountered.

Therefore, the process goal of establishing a facilitative relationship can be described as a specific level of communication which is far more intense than that of most other human relationships. If the client speaks about things, or himself, in a manner in which he would speak to most people, then he is probably not operating in the context of a good and appropriate therapeutic relationship. In contrast, if the client speaks about himself in a manner in which he would not do so with most other people, then there is some indication that the relationship is especially strong and favorable.

Frequent use of CRRLs to affect is highly appropriate throughout the establishment of the therapeutic relationship. CRRLs to affect demonstrate effectively to the client the counselor's warm and empathic qualities. Such responses not only indicate, "I understand you," but also, "I respect you and have listened to your ideas with acceptance." Once the counselor has communicated these qualities and the client has become aware of them, the counselor has already made a major and favorable impact on the client, and has set himself up to have a major and favorable impact in future sessions.

THE GOAL OF THE FACILITATIVE RELATIONSHIP   *The facilitative relationship is not a goal in itself;* rather, it is a stage in the process necessary for the important steps which follow. The establishment of this relationship, therefore, is purposive and goal directed in aiding the development of the counseling process. Once this relationship has been established, the counselor is in a position to evaluate: (1) what it is that the client wants to get out of the counseling process; (2) what it is that is motivating the client to seek assistance in light of what it is he desires to change; (3) what strategies are most relevant to the client and his situation in helping him to change; and (4) what new learnings must be mastered by the client in order to insure the success of the new behavior as it is related to his goal for the process.

The client, who speaks about himself and the world in which he lives in a deep, meaningful manner, must realize that the counselor understands, accepts, and cares for him, is genuine and honest in his relationship with him, and is a professional person who is capable of helping him. *This verbal behavior of the client is the goal of this stage of the process,* and is the goal of counseling itself. The establishment of a facilitative relationship is, therefore, the most important ingredient in this process.

THE CRITERIA FOR ASSESSING THE FACILITATIVE RELATION-SHIP   In order for the counselor to assess his success in establishing a therapeutic relationship, the following criteria are offered, in question form:

1. Did I understand what the client was saying?
2. Did the client realize I understood him?
3. Did I see the world of the client through the client's eyes?
4. Did the client realize that I perceived *with* him?
5. Was I warm, compassionate, and interested in the client; and did I demonstrate this by my demeanor?
6. Did the client perceive my desire to be warm and interested in him?

7. What emotions am I feeling toward my client, and how are these emotions influencing my actions toward him?
8. Are there certain things I am reluctant to say to my client? If so, what implications does that inhibition have for our relationship?
9. On what important issues do the values, beliefs, and opinions of my client differ from mine? Are those differences influencing my ability to accept him?
10. Was that person in the counseling session really me? Was I genuine and honest as a person?
11. Was the client aware that I was genuine and honest with him?
12. Did I behave in a professional manner, offering my services and my help where it was appropriate?
13. Did the client perceive me as a professional person capable of and desirous of helping him?
14. In brief, did I establish a facilitative relationship with the client as demonstrated by my behavior and perceived by the client?
15. Did I meet the goal of this relationship: helping the client to talk about those personally relevant things which the client felt were necessary for me to understand him.

Very often the client will say that he has never spoken this way to anyone before. Sometimes, it is appropriate for counselor feedback concerning the relationship, to ask, "To how many people have you spoken the way you've spoken to me?" It is necessary, however, for the counselor to be able to follow through on such questions, depending upon the answer.

SUMMARY

The relationship stage in the counseling process is begun as early as possible, but not later than the beginning of the second session. The process goal of this stage is to establish a facilitative relationship in which the client sees the counselor as a person who deeply understands him, who accepts him fully, who is genuine, who is capable of offering the kind of professional help needed, and who can be completely trusted. The counselor must behave in such ways as to attain relationship-related goals and must avoid behaving in such ways as to interfere with the attainment of those goals. To do that, the counselor must continually examine his beliefs, attitudes, and feelings toward the client and assess whether they are congruent with the qualities which must be communicated to the client. Incongruities must be worked through if the counselor is to be effective. Counselor reflective response leads (CRRLs) are especially valuable in communicating understanding, acceptance, and professional competency.

Suggestions for helping counselors enhance their empathic sensitivity are offered, and criteria to help counselors assess the strength of their relationship with their clients are presented.

CASE OF BETTY Betty is an attractive twenty-six-year-old woman. She and her husband were referred for individual counseling. The following typescript is taken from the first session. Up to this point, she has talked only about the difficulty in general terms, does not seem to know how to proceed, or what to expect from counseling. She stated that her husband had asked for a divorce the previous week, although they would prefer to "save" the marriage.

The first segment is thirty minutes into the session; the second segment is the last ten minutes of the first session.

Segment One

> *Client* 1: I know the person on the outside real well but I don't understand myself inside. I guess that's what makes it hard to, ah, more difficult to talk about 'cause I don't know that person. I should. I mean it's me. I know the person inside has . . . a lot of misgivings, misunderstanding of things, and ah . . . I mean that ah . . . seems like the little person inside got locked up. When or where, I'm not sure. Maybe when I was little and I didn't get things

I wanted. Maybe when I ran off and got married and got hurt, mistreated, somewhere along the way, it just all built up to this. The little person still holds a lot of *hate.* Instead of getting rid of it like it should have been, it just, I guess it's all spilling out on my husband now. I don't know. It's hard to understand.

Counselor 1: Would you like to talk about that? The feelings you have of having hurt, and the hate?

Comments: A very effective empathic response which helps the client explore her feelings. The counselor did two very important things at this important choice point situation. First, he chose to take the discussion into the area of the client's feelings. Second, he accurately identified some of the feelings the client was experiencing—hurt and hate. Notice the favorable impact this strategy has with Betty as is indicated by what she subsequently says. As you read what she says, try to identify overt feelings directly stated, and covert feelings implied by the kind of situation she describes.

Client 2: Oh, boy! Now, that we could write a book on. We really could. I'm the oldest of four children. My mother was pretty much; she wasn't in the best of health. Sometimes I feel that I was made to grow up a little too soon rather than what I should've. Did a lot a things I thought she was capable of doing if she would just remove herself from a chair once in awhile. We didn't get along very well. In fact, she and I stay away from each other quite a bit. She got, gave me free rein. Do what you want to do as long as you get this much done. If you don't do that, well, then you don't do anything else. Her and my daddy was getting into it over me. I learned like any kid, you know, get the one who'll do the most for you real fast. If she'll let you do it, butter her up, and if he'll let you, butter him up. But it was miserable; it was uncomfortable. There was quite a bit of fighting and ah, I just wanted out of there, so I got out. But what I thought was bad was, I guess now when I look back at it, was pretty much heaven because I walked into something that was a whole lot worse. I married a man who'd been married before. It started out like any other marriage, two people happy. I was pregnant when we got married. And whether this, they say this is a mark against a marriage to begin with, I don't know, and my parents hated him. They didn't like him. They had thrown him out a couple of times when he came to the house. So we just galloped around the country like we didn't belong anywhere. We never had anything. When Hank, who is my oldest boy, came along, and things, well they calmed down you know, and ah, I got pregnant with my second one. Neither one of us was ready to accept that. I know this for a fact. It took them about an hour and a half to calm me down after the doctor told me I was expecting him. There's only twelve months between them, and ah, I don't think my husband was ready to accept the responsibility of a full family. He started running around, and I started nagging, you know. So I'm pregnant. So what. I can go just as well as anybody else, and ah. . . . First thing I know he's taken off down in the country with who but his first wife. Joy, you know. I'm six months' pregnant, no money to pay the rent and he's galloped down the countryside somewhere. I carry scars from him. This is one [*indicates lip*]. And ah, the youngest boy, well he's pretty settled now but when he was eleven months' old he couldn't go to sleep at night from being so nervous and tied up. Things were quite bad for him because it seems like his daddy took quite a bit of anger out on him, too, and ah. . . . Things just got worse, you know; first thing I know I'm in court fighting him for the kids, and found out through evidently somebody who shouldn't have said anything, that neither one of us was going to get them. And my mother and daddy came to the scene, good ole mother and daddy, and all, but ah . . . I don't seem to be able to relax without the fear that someday it's gonna start all over, and ah, I don't like any part of it. Sammy has a habit of patting me on the back and like I've told him, I said if he's been beat and knocked around like I have, you wouldn't be able to take that either. It just gets to me. He's been pretty good last couple of weeks; he's not so bad. He doesn't insist on giving me his little love pats anymore. Which is all they are, just love pats. Now I know without a doubt there have been some times when he would've liked to knocked me flat right then, you know, but he never has, never has attempted to, and he says he never will. If it gets to the point that I have to think like that and act like that, he says, I definitely will walk out and call it quits. But I haven't been able to accept a lot of this, a . . . sometimes I just set back and wait, you know, when's it all going to start all over. When's it all going to explode in my face. Things can't go on like this forever. They just . . . this is my innermost thought. Things don't go smooth like this all the time.

Counselor 2: You're sort of waiting for. . . .

Comments: Many people who experience the kind and intensity of stress experienced by Betty want desperately just to communicate their misery to someone else. All they want from that other person is to know he is paying close attention and listening carefully. What impact do you think occurred for Betty as a result of communicating her feelings to the counselor?

Client 3: . . . the keg of dynamite to blow up. And when it did, it was over something so simple. Oh, I realized it was coming. That's why I took the steps I did.

Segment Two

Client 11:   It's hard to understand why things happen the way they do, and then try to understand yourself, too. I'm pretty bad on that part. It looks better.

Comments: Reflective response lead.

Counselor 11:   It is difficult to get to know oneself, if we ever really do.

Client 12:   I don't expect to live the rest of my life without things happening because this isn't possible, really. There are going to be bad times, there are going to be good times, and ah, I feel that, just inside of me, that where there's a marriage and there are strong enough ties between a man and his wife, they can just about do anything they'd like to. They can make anything work, and ah, just like I told Sammy, just as long as we stay out of the bedroom, we can whip the world. But when we get in there, we start fighting. So . . . I don't really fear him. I, as I said before, I think it's just that he's a man and men *hurt*. So here again, it's hard to understand.

Counselor 12:   I can understand why you would feel that way.

Comments: Statement of understanding and support.

Client 13:   I don't understand, you know, why really, why should I take this out on him. 'Cause he's been so good to me and so understanding and, really, he's put up with an awful lot. Understand that much of it now. I don't know, here again, the way I feel, too, is that I say that I have three children, but I have had actually four. This is hard to understand, not really, once I tell you. As far as anybody around me knows, I have three children. I have one that falls between the youngest boy and the youngest girl, and by rights, I have the right to say he's mine, but he's adopted out. And that was one of those kind of deals in which you get involved. You're looking for happiness, and you think you have it and everything looks promising, and you think he's gonna marry you and the first thing you know, you've got so involved that . . . there you are. So I get burned and he backs out and takes off. So here, I have the responsibility of my two children, but I'm carrying the third child who has no father. He takes off down the country somewhere, and ah, against my better judgment, ah, I still feel that I shouldn't have done it, but I had no help, not really. My folks refused even the thought of my bringing the baby home. So I went ahead and he was adopted out.

Counselor 13:   You felt very much alone.

Comments: Reflective response lead. Perhaps the client was also feeling guilty about abandoning her baby. What might have been the impact if the counselor had responded: "Putting your baby up for adoption must have been a very hard thing for you to do. Do you still think about that baby sometimes, and wonder if you did the right thing?"

Client 14: I was. Very much. I was. Well, the people at the home for unwed mothers were very understanding, but they, ah, they knew I had two children staying with my parents, and ah, but what they didn't know was, ah, that my parents wouldn't let me come there to live till I could get back on my feet. So it sticks in my mind that I had no other way to go but that way 'cause I had no place to take a new baby and I really had nothing to offer him. So, ah, then I got pregnant with Kim after me and Sammy went to Alaska. We were pretty happy about it, and here I had no trouble, you know, no trouble, and suddenly she's born half a month early and we almost lose her. It was three weeks before we could bring her home. Still, the doctor said it was just one of those freak things. Her system was poisoned and they didn't know what caused it because, you know the military, they, they're pretty strict. They make you go and get yourself checked and make sure that you stay checked and stay healthy. They said it was no fault of mine, but still, you know, it just, I felt like somewhere along the line I'd lose her, too, and be punished for all the things that had happened in the past. So, so I guess it's all somewhere, all in the same pot.

I won't turn loose and trust him like I
should; 'cause I don't know, I should
know, but I don't know what to expect
from him. I don't think he would run
around on me. I have no fear of that
but I'm afraid that if things keep like
they are, even if he stayed, you know,
that this is the way it would end up. I
don't want that and I don't think he
does, or we'd neither one be here. So
. . . that's the terrible messed up past,
and somewhere, somehow, it all works
into the problems that are now.

Counselor 14:   Of course it does. Well, Betty, I think we
can work on this problem together. I
think I can help you. Betty, would you
like to come in two times a week?

Comments: Closing of initial session.

Client 15:   Okay; anyway you want to set it up. I'm
willing. I can.

Counselor 15:   Okay; let's see what John and your husband are going to set up for appoint-
ments.

CASE OF PAULA   Paula was referred to the Counseling Center
by a lawyer she had contacted because of a civil suit brought
against her by another party. Her husband is an Army enlisted man
stationed in Germany. He had heard of Paula's difficulties through
correspondence with his mother. The client feels her marriage is
breaking up. She is very distraught and feels guilty about her past
behavior toward her husband. This typescript begins a few minutes after the start of the fourth session. In this case, note especially how Paula reacts to the CRRLs at Counselor 4, 5, and 6. Each
time she provides feedback to the counselor that he has understood her. It is apparent that the counselor was listening and understanding. If he were not, he could not possibly have responded

the way he did, particularly at Counselor 4. This response seemed particularly impactful because it helped both focus on the real conflict Paula was experiencing but having trouble communicating.

> *Counselor:* What would you do if you weren't communicating with Mike through letters? If he were here, how would you talk to him?
>
> *Client* 1: Well, it would have had to start long before this very minute, and I would have had to tell him that I know there's something wrong with me, that he's been overly fair and I haven't been, and that I need help and my main goal right now is for him to help me and to get better and to have a family and if he'll help me that's all I want. But you see I've done that in letters and it doesn't work.
>
> *Counselor* 1: What happens?
>
> *Client* 2: Mike . . . well, it's his mother again. Uh, I told him that I was coming for help. My mom even wrote him and told him. Well, he might write and say, "What'd they . . . what'd they have to say today?" End of the thing, you know. Then he'd start in with the rest of it. He just . . . he acts like he doesn't care. I mean that's . . . that's why I'm sure that it's over because he used to write me and tell me—you know— I'd say—you know—I drove here and there, it might just be around the block. "Paula, please be careful when you drive. If anything ever happened to you . . . to you then there'd be no point for me to live." Boy, he couldn't care less now whether I . . . in fact it'd

probably be easier on him if I did go out and kill myself. Then he wouldn't have to worry about me any more.

Counselor 2: The picture has really changed from one where he wanted very much to have a good marriage and you gave him the impression at times that you didn't really care and you weren't sure that you did yourself, and now that you have decided that you really want this marriage to work, you aren't sure that he still wants it to.

Client 3: Yeah.

Counselor 3: You almost feel as if it's too late.

Client 4: What'd you do when you feel like it's too late for something; I mean, do you just give up or what? I mean, how do you know when somethin' is really over? I mean . . . this isn't like having boyfriends. Susie [Paula's sister] has laughed about it even recently. I used to have more boyfriends than you could imagine and they'd call all the time you know—come over—you know my mother always had a house full of guys, you know. My sister didn't date much, but I had all kinds of guys, you know—we'd be—and I'd never get serious. We were always doing crazy things all the time. We'd be out tobogganing or making cakes in the kitchen or something—just crazy things and so Susie used to make the comment if I'd decided I didn't like a certain guy anymore or if he decided he didn't like me, that's fine because tomorrow I'd be out looking for somebody else. And so, I never had to worry about before whether, well now, is this really over, should I forget it or not, because I never really cared about anybody before that way, but now I do. And I'm not smart enough to know I guess when something is really over and I guess I—I want to know if something, if it's really over then I'd better start changing my life and working around it to plan for something else because I mean what's the point in trying to hang onto something you really don't have . . . I guess.

Counselor 4:   You know, Paula, what's coming through to me, and I may be wrong, is that on the one hand you still have some hope, knowing how Mike has been in the past, you can't really feel that he would give it up so easily, and you wanta do anything you can to work through this and to make a good marriage; and on the other hand, you're almost inclined to say, "Well, I'd better just decide now that it's not going to work and reconcile myself to this fact rather than really make an all-out attempt to keep him and then not keep him and have to admit that I couldn't."

Client 5:   You've put it beautifully, you just put it beautifully. That's—that's what I've been trying to say, but I can't say things like you or my mom can, you know, I don't know how to say it. You just said it beautifully and that is why I go out at night; that's not—that's why I don't go home because there's nothing to go home to. I . . . I write Mike letters every night at work. I wrote him one yesterday morning when I got that . . . that one letter but I wrote to him last night again and I said, "Here I am at work," I said. "I wrote you a long letter today but it doesn't seem right not to write to you because I'm at work." I write him a letter every night at work. The bellboys laugh about it because, "Well, there she goes, writin' a letter." Some nights it's nine pages, ya know, and they think this is really funny. "What do you say in nine pages?" I don't know —you know—if I, if you asked me I really couldn't tell you—you know— how I fill up nine pages. But that . . . that's my only link with trying to hold him, I think is my letter because I have no other. And then, so why not go out? There's no . . . there's no point not to because it's for sure that if he divorces me, I'm not gonna sit at home every night. I mean I wouldn't be normal if I did and I know that because I've got girl friends who've been divorced or husbands were killed or something they don't sit at home every night and I wouldn't expect them to. I mean it may take 'em a while to come —you know—to come around to going out again, but then they have a good time. I guess I . . . I'm just . . . I don't know how I feel. I know I want him back but wanting him and getting him are two different things.

Counselor 5:   So you're almost saying, "I'll reject you before you have a chance to reject me."

Client 6:   Yes, and I've done that very, very many times. Now I told you, you know, if a guy decided he didn't want me or if I decided I didn't want him, I don't think I ever really gave a guy a chance to say, "I don't wanta go out with you any more." I'd say it first. I'd feel it coming and then I'd take care of it, 'cause I never wanted to be, I never wanted a guy to think, "Oh, I quit going with her" or something, you know. I always was the one to say, just quit dating him or something. But if Mike . . . yesterday when I first read that letter, I was laying in . . . Susie brought the letter in to me and I was laying in bed and I lay there and read it. I just laid there and I didn't know what I was gonna do. I thought, gosh, it's really over. He doesn't believe a thing I've ever told him. Then all of a sudden I got mad, and I thought, by damn I've lied to you before but I'm not now! And I want you to believe me now. You know, don't ever tell . . . don't ever tell people a fib because when you do and you get caught at it then the next time nobody believes you.

Counselor 6:   You sorta get a reputation that's hard to live down.

Client 7:   That's right.

Counselor 7:   Well, it seems to me at this point that it might be helpful for you to do some thinking this next week, and attempt to come to some decision as to whether you really want to go all out to save your marriage, with the possibility of being rejected by Mike, but also with the possibility of saving the marriage, or, on the other hand, if you wanta end it now by throwing him out before he has a chance to throw you out—to save your own pride, or your own feelings of hurt, etc., uh, maybe you should do some thinking about how important it is to you to continue the relationship with Mike. And then from there, after you make this decision this will determine what we do in the future, which direction we go in, what we do here.

Client 8: Boy, I appreciate you telling me that. I guess I already know my decision on that because—you know I've been thinking around it, you know. I . . . I've never really come right out and thought to myself what you just said but I've been thinking around it you know now if I do this you know and if I do that—but—I want him. I'll swear I've had . . . my sister's written to him, my mother's written to him . . . and before I didn't care if anybody wrote to him, I thought, well, I'll say everything that's needed—you know—that I need to say. But—I truly want him back. That's all there is to it. Time's about up today, isn't it?

Counselor 8: Yes, it is. Well, give it some thought this week and be sure.

Client 9: It's gonna be completely up to me. It really is. I mean maybe the decision itself isn't up to me, 'cause Mike will be the one in the end to make that decision.

Counselor 9: Well, he will make his decision. What you decide to do is up to you.

Client 10: Well, what I mean is, you know, if I decide I want him and I do everything, it's gonna be him to say, "Well, you've won or you've lost." You know, this is it. But it's going to be up to me to pattern my life, and how I plan to keep him. I mean I'm gonna have to stay home and I'm gonna have to—this is ... this is gonna be the hardest decision right there—is to ... to make up my mind to go home every night and to ... to wait on him.

Counselor 10:   Well, maybe it isn't the decision that will be the hardest but the carrying it out. If you decide you wanta do certain things then getting yourself to do it might be the problem.

Client 11:   'Cause I can make a bunch of decisions but whether I do it or not is two different things. Like my mom—she said the other night—and she didn't know she was hurting me when she said it 'cause we were just kidding around— but I said, I was showing her a picture ... I had a picture; she said, "I wanta see it." I said, "No, you'll tear it up." She said, "No I won't." She said, "Let me see it." I said, "Do you promise?" She said, "Well . . ." and she said, "Well," she said, "I've asked you to make me a lot of promises." She didn't realize really what she was saying, but it got through to me because I have ... I've made her a lot of promises that I haven't followed through on and she thinks in her own mind, which is o.k. 'cause she's really trying to do right by me, that I made her a promise to come here and I'm keeping it for her. But she's wrong, I'm keeping it for me. And if that's selfish, then I'll be selfish the rest of my life because I want to be a good wife and I want to straighten out and—it's not gonna help her for—the only person it's gonna help is me. I mean it'll help her to an extent to know that I'm o.k. and that I'm living the life I should, but I'm only doing this for me and nobody else.

Counselor 11:   Well I think this is as it should be. This is why you should be here, not because someone else wants you to but because you wanta be.

SUGGESTIONS FOR
FURTHER READING

Berenson, B. G. and Carkhuff, R. R.
   1967   *Sources of Gain in Counseling and Psychotherapy.* New York: Holt, Rinehart and Winston.

Buber, M.
   1937   *I and Thou,* trans. R. G. Smith. Edinburgh: T. Clark.

Carkhuff, R. R.
   1969   *Helping and Human Relations; Selection and Training,* vol. 1; *Practice and Research,* vol. 2. New York: Holt, Rinehart and Winston.

Carkhuff, R R. and Berenson, B. G.
   1967   *Beyond Counseling and Therapy.* New York: Holt, Rinehart and Winston.

Frankl, V. E.
   1955   *From Death Camp to Existentialism,* trans. L. Lasch. Boston: Beacon Press.

Fromm, E.
   1956   *The Art of Loving.* New York: Harper and Row.
   1961   *Man for Himself.* New York: Holt, Rinehart and Winston.
   1962   *Beyond the Chains of Illusion.* New York: Pocket Books.

Goldstein, A. P.
   1962   *Therapist-Patient Expectancies in Psychotherapy.* New York: Pergamon Press.

Jourard, S. M.
   1964   *The Transparent Self.* Princeton, N. J.: Van Nostrand.

Kell, B. L. and Mueller, W. J.
   1966   *Impact and Change: A Study of Counseling Relationships.* New York: Appleton-Century-Crofts.

Rogers, C. R.
   1951   *Client Centered Therapy.* Boston: Houghton Mifflin.
   1961   *On Becoming a Person.* Boston: Houghton Mifflin.

Truax, C. B. and Carkhuff, R. R.
   1967   *Toward Effective Counseling and Psychotherapy.* Chicago: Aldine Press.

Chapter 5   Goal Identification and Determination of Counseling Strategies

The related notions that the behavior of both client and counselor is purposive and goal directed were developed in Chapter 2. Also developed were the following: that in order to attain certain outcome goals, certain process goals must first be attained; and that the effectiveness of counseling is directly related to the counselor's ability to describe both outcome and process goals and to develop counseling strategies to attain those goals. These related notions become especially important in the third stage of counseling—the goal identification stage. It is during this stage when client and counselor systematically identify and evaluate the outcome goals of counseling and where the counselor begins to formulate process goals for counseling and strategies to achieve these goals.

This stage begins only after the effective and facilitative kind of counseling relationship discussed in the previous chapter has been established—usually somewhere around the third or fourth session. Thus, it is appropriate to identify the establishment of an effective relationship as an important process goal which must occur early, if later counseling goals are to be attained.

This third stage—the goal and strategy identification stage—may be seen as having four important and interrelated components.

1. The establishment of target or outcome goals of counseling.
2. The determination and consideration of client characteristics which might influence the counselor's strategy.
3. The thinking through of those process goals which must be attained if later outcome goals are to be reached and the sequence in which those process goals might occur.
4. The development of a strategy (or plan of action) to be implemented to help the client achieve the identified goal.

GOAL IDENTIFICATION   Describing the goals of the counseling process is frequently a difficult task. Outcome goals are often described in such terms as self-exploration, self-understanding, greater self-awareness, and self-actualization. These terms are too vague, unclear, and unspecified to be satisfactory. The outcome goals of the counseling process must be described in behavioral terms. *Counseling can be described as successful when, and only when, some kind of change of observable behavior has occurred.*

A client may report that as a result of counseling he feels better, has more confidence, and more fully understands himself and his world. While these changes may in fact have occurred, they are not descriptions of behavior change, and, hence, not adequate indicators of counseling success. On the other hand, if a client were to say, "I feel a greater sense of confidence as a result of counseling. This has had a real influence in the way I function with people. In contrast to the way I functioned before, I now find myself engaging in a sustained conversation with people; my speaking is more fluent, I can more strongly assert my positions on issues even where I am aware others will disagree; I look straight at people when I am talking to them instead of at the floor; I smile more frequently, and I have stopped that continual pattern of saying negative things about myself," then the client has described changes in his overt behavior which was what he and the counselor were trying to attain. While it cannot be certain that such changes were the result of counseling, at least there is an indication that favorable changes did occur and it is quite possible that it was, in fact, a result of the counseling intervention. The important point to realize is that counseling success must be described in terms of behavioral change.

While that principle holds in general for all counseling intervention, the *specific* behavior changes, and the counseling strategies implemented to achieve those changes, is specific to each client. This statement is also consistent with the counselor's involvement in the decision-making process. A major service many counselors provide is in helping clients make decisions about future plans and actions. In schools, many counselors try to help students decide which career field to enter after graduation. For other students, it is what institution of higher education to attend and in which potential discipline to major. Other students are seriously trying to decide whether they should stay in school or drop out. For students who come to a counselor for help in making such types of decisions, the counseling goal is to help the student decide on the course of action that *he* believes will be in his best future interest. Counseling success is still described in terms of some kind of behavior change. It may be a statement to the effect, "As a result of our discussions, I am much more clear about what course of action will be in my future best interest." The ultimate criterion in decision-making cases, however, occurs when the client states the decision at which he has arrived, then actually takes action to implement the choice he has made, and, upon follow-up, communicates to the counselor that the decision he made turned out to be the wisest he could have made. In the next chapter, a more complete analysis of the decision-making process will be presented.

Most people who write about counseling see counselors as people helping others to look at their values, beliefs, attitudes (especially their attitudes toward themselves), and philosophy of life. This sort of process is of value only if it will help the client attain the goals he came to the counselor to reach. For some clients, this may be an essential and valuable process. An example might be where a client comes to a counselor and states that his goal is to work through his philosophy of life and resolve discrepancies he is perceiving; counselors in schools, incidentally, see relatively few such clients. For other clients, such activity is not instrumental in helping them attain the goals for which they came to the counselor and, hence, cannot be justified. An example here might be a client having a debilitating phobia, such as test anxiety. For such a client, systematic desensitization may be a more viable intervention strategy. As shall be developed more fully in the next chapter, such a strategy involves little or no "self-understanding" as the term has been traditionally used in the counseling literature. The point to be made is that the counselor must implement those strategies which will be instrumental in helping his client attain his counseling goals. If value clarification or philosophy analysis is instrumental to attaining his stated counseling goals, such activity is justifiable. If such activity is not instrumental to achieving the goals of counseling, it cannot be justified. Such activity may very well be instrumental in helping a certain client with certain kinds of decisions. It is less likely to be justifiable in helping clients work through their fears and phobias.

COUNSELOR TACTING RESPONSE LEADS (CTRLs)   The manner in which the counselor responds to his client is functionally related to the successful attainment of counseling goals. Certain counselor responses are especially instrumental at specific stages of the counseling process to facilitate counseling movement. The counselor reflective response lead, as previously identified, is especially instrumental during the relationship-establishing stage. A counselor verbal response which is especially instrumental during the goal-setting stage is the counselor tacting response lead (CTRL). The intent or purpose of the CTRL is to help the client discuss abstract concepts in more specific terms, or to associate significant behavioral events with certain environmental circumstances. Effective use of CTRLs will help the client to be more specific about what he is saying, and thereby, to attach new and more accurate meanings to what he is saying.

Such activity is essential in establishing and clarifying the goals of counseling. Clients frequently are unclear about the goals they have for counseling. If counseling is to be successful the goals of counseling must be clearly described. Clients frequently recognize that they are unhappy and are experiencing stress. They, therefore, come to the counselor for help in alleviating their stress and unhappiness. The concepts they use, however, to describe their difficulties are frequently too vague and abstract to clearly describe the goals of counseling.

For some clients, dissatisfactory behaviors occur in certain types of situations. In facilitating some sort of behavior change, it is essential for both client and counselor to learn the types of situations in which the dissatisfactory behavior occurs. For example, a client comes in and says he "gets mad all the time." The term "mad" needs to be defined. A CTRL is highly instrumental in achieving that goal. "Tell me what you mean when you say you get 'mad.' " Further, it is essential to learn under what situations he is most likely to get mad (or as he may later define this term, "to express anger toward adults"). Thus, another CTRL would be instrumental here: "Tell me a specific time when you expressed especially strong anger toward adults." Clearly, this CTRL is trying to identify *situations* in which the dissatisfactory behavior occurs. Upon the client's response, "When my father wouldn't let me join the basketball team," the counselor may follow with yet another tacting response: "Tell me about another time when you expressed anger this strongly to an adult." The client may respond by saying, "The time when my teacher refused to let me sit next to my friend, Tom." The counselor would then be able to identify situations in which adults blocked the client from attaining goals which were important to him. With this, the counselor could more clearly identify appropriate ways to proceed. Such interaction is essential to establishing counseling goals in four ways:

1. CTRLs aid both the counselor and the client to operationally define the terms the client is using. The following examples are used to demonstrate this. A client response is followed by two verbal interactions, A and B. Interaction A is a non-CTRL counselor use and Interaction B is a CTRL counselor use.

Client:	I just can't seem to concentrate. It's really affecting my school work. My grades are slipping and I know I'm not doing well,

but no matter how hard I try, I can't concentrate.

Interaction A

> *Counselor:* This is affecting your school work.
> *Client:* Yes, my grades are slipping—particularly in algebra.

Interaction B

> *Counselor:* Tell me what you mean when you say you are unable to concentrate.
> *Client:* Well . . . I daydream about things that I'd rather not think about.

Clearly, the result of Interaction A would be talking about grades in school, etc. The result of Interaction B, on the other hand, is the client talking about his daydreaming which is likely to be more important in establishing a goal for the counseling process.

2. CTRLs aid both the client and the counselor to experience vicariously the significant happenings and circumstances surrounding some specific previous event. This will lead to a better understanding of the client's behavior in that previous significant experience. The following example is offered to illustrate this principle:

> *Client:* I just don't seem to be able to do anything right. No matter how hard I try, it's never good enough. Somebody is always criticizing the way I've done it. Nobody ever tells me I've done anything right, and now I feel like I can't do anything right at all.

Interaction A

> *Counselor:* This is upsetting to you.
> *Client:* Yes. I don't feel like I can do anything right at all.

Interaction B

>*Counselor:* Tell me about a time when someone criti-
>cized you.
>
>*Client:* Last evening when my father came home
>from work, I had cut the grass in the
>afternoon and he found fault with that.
>He always finds fault with whatever I do.

Interaction A results in more talk concerning the client's inability to "do anything right." Interaction B results in the client talking about an event that has happened. This event is the environmental prop from which clarification will come concerning the "nobody," "always," "anything" and aid in the determination of the counseling goal.

Clearly, if a counselor's task is to help his client acquire more rewarding behavior, learn to cope more effectively with difficult situations, modify certain behaviors which are maladaptive under certain situations, then it is important that both client and counselor clearly understand the events, circumstances and situations in which these new, more rewarding behaviors are to occur. Clear descriptions of the circumstances with which the client would like to cope more effectively or behave in a more rewarding manner may be seen as a necessary process goal in counseling, and CTRLs are especially instrumental counselor responses for attaining this process goal.

3. CTRLs aid both the counselor and client to vicariously experience, or to express once again, any physiological reactions and changes *at the time of* the specific experience, leading to a clarification and better understanding of client behavior and feelings in the situation. The following example is offered:

>*Client:* I'm scared. I'm always scared. I don't know
>what it is, but I'm always nervous. I'm

nervous about everything, especially when I go to bed at night.

Interaction A

> *Counselor:* This is causing you some concern.
>
> *Client:* Yeah. I don't like to be scared like this.

Interaction B

> *Counselor:* Tell me how you feel inside of you when you go to bed.
>
> *Client:* It's not that I feel any differently, it's just that I know I'm scared, but I don't have any "butterflies" in my stomach, if that's what you mean.

The type of clarifying information concerning what the client is saying in Interaction B, as a result of the CTRL the counselor used, will assist both client and counselor in goal identification.

4. By the continued use of CTRLs, the counselor will help the client to use tacting responses. Over a period of time, the client will be able to respond with specific situations, feelings, and physical reactions to props in his environment. This continued use of CTRLs will help the client to form a concept which will enable him to compare and contrast his behavior in various settings, and under different conditions. The following example is illustrative:

> *Client:* Elevators. I never go on them. Like I've said, I haven't ridden one in months. I always walk while everyone else rides. We went to Chicago since I saw you last. Everybody went to the restaurant on the top floor. I didn't go; my stomach would have been in knots.

Interaction A

> *Counselor:* This really "bugs" you.
>
> *Client:* Darn right.

Interaction B

> *Counselor:* As we have talked, now, would these feel-
> ings about elevators apply to anything
> else?
>
> *Client:* Well . . . let's see. . . . to airplanes, and
> sometimes trains, and buses. . . . I'd say,
> to an extent, almost anything that I can't
> get out of when I want to.

One can see the difference in the direction the client
is taking as a result of counselor use of CTRL in Interaction B. The ultimate goal identification by the client is
made easier and more effective by the counselor's
CTRL.

In summary, a CTRL is a counselor lead which facilitates the
client's talk in making contact with an environmental prop. Helping the client think and talk specifically concerning events, occasions, feelings, etc., will lead to the identification of the goals for
counseling (both process and outcome), as well as help the counselor to better understand and appreciate the client, the client's
needs, and the client's perceptions of himself and the world in
which he lives.

DETERMINATION OF CLIENT INPUT   Following the identification
and establishment of counseling goals, the counselor must make
some assessment of the physical and psychological input which
the client brings to the counseling process. There are some tools
and techniques to be used in this assessment. The necessity and
extent of the assessment, however, is directly dependent upon the
established goal. For example, vocational planning and decision
making would require considerably more client input assessment
than a study habit problem, but less than a problem in the area of
personality disorder. The use of various tools is dependent upon
the counselor's level of training, educational background, and
experience.

Physical Assessment   If, for any reason, the counselor suspects
some *physical* incapacity or disability which might hinder the cli-

ent's development toward his desired goal, then a referral to a physician is essential. Basically, a referral for a medical checkup and diagnosis is appropriate for any of the following reasons: (1) the counselor suspects that the goal or target behavior is beyond the client's potential, due to some physical cause; (2) the counselor suspects that the problem identified has as its cause something physical; (3) the counselor suspects that the problem can be treated best through medical intervention; (4) the counselor believes that a medical report is necessary for continuing the counseling process.

Psychological Assessment and Diagnosis   Assessment refers to the process of describing the attributes and characteristics of the client. Assessment is always based on what the counselor observes of the client's behavior. Sometimes this observation occurs informally in the course of the counseling sessions. As the counselor listens to the client he makes *inferences* about the client based on what the client has said. For example, if the client were to say, "I just never seem to be able to do anything right. I can't seem to make friends; I'm doing poorly in school; I'm overweight; my parents are *always* criticizing me. Even worse, my younger sister is more popular and does better in school. My parents really favor her," the counselor, then, might infer that the client sees himself as inferior and worthless, and whose self-esteem is low. At other times, this observation is done more formally through the use of various kinds of test instruments.

Sometimes assessment is based on whether certain characteristics are present or absent. At other times, dimensions or continua are used to characterize the client. When these are used, assessment is generally based on how this client compares to other people, for example, people of his own age, his own sex, and people in the same situation as the client. Some of the more important dimensions on which counselors base their assessments will be described.

Level of Intellectual Functioning or Intellectual Development   The concept "intelligence" is deceptively simple, for it has many meanings and connotations: a numerical score on a test purported to measure "intelligence"; the ability to think abstractly; the ability to survive in a hostile environment; the ability to solve difficult problems. A variety of tests, group and individual, are available which purport to assess intellectual development. In counseling situations, counselors frequently base their inferences about their client's level of intellectual development on such factors as the vocabulary the client uses, the correctness of his grammar, his demonstrated ability to think in abstract terms, etc. Some counselors believe that assessment of a client's level of intellectual development is essential, for their counseling strategy will be based on this assessment. Thus, their strategy with children would be different from their strategy with adults because the two differ with respect to their level of intellectual development. Other counselors believe that level of intellectual development is not related to their counseling strategy, and, hence, such an assessment is unimportant.

Emotional States   Human emotions are vital factors of human behavior, and as such, are considered to be important components in the counseling process. Helping clients to more fully understand their feelings about important experiences and situations is frequently considered an essential process goal for many clients. Since this is so, most people who write about counseling believe it is important to understand, and be sensitive to, the dominant feelings the client expresses, and to particular situations which will influence the client to experience certain of these strong feelings. Particularly important emotions which counselors are sensitive to are: anxiety or some sort of fear, anger, hostility, hate, some form of aggression, depression, sadness, or some form of misery, guilt, and happiness or joy.

The counselor may ask himself many questions concerning the emotional behavior of his client:

1. Are there particular feelings which are more predominant than others in this client's functioning? Does he have an unusually strong tendency to blow his stack or to be depressed?

2. Are there particularly "critical situations" which will influence the client to have particularly intense emotional reactions?

3. Life space is full of potentially emotion-eliciting situations.

Compared to other clients, how does this client respond to these key "emotion-eliciting" situations? For example, when a peer expresses strong verbal hostility, how does the client respond emotionally? How does he respond to criticism from a person in an authoritative position?

4. Emotions can be described along an "intensity" dimension, from low to strong intensity. Given the same frustrating situation, for example, some clients will express mild annoyance, others will express strong, violent rage. When a particular client feels something or expresses an emotion, the counselor may well ask, "How intense was that emotional reaction?" Being sensitive to client feelings means responding not only to the particular kind of emotion, but the *intensity* of the emotion as well.

Since a client's emotions are not always clearly observable, counselors must infer about a client's emotions by what is observable: his verbal and nonverbal behavior in the presence of the counselor and his description of important situations. Recalling the concepts developed in Chapter 2 will help counselors assess the kind and quality of emotion experienced by his client. Thus, when a client discusses a situation and it is appropriate to describe that situation as "frustrating," the counselor can hypothesize that the client probably responded with anger, anxiety, or depression in that situation. Some form of anger is an especially frequent response to frustrating situations. When a client describes situations in which his safety, security, or well-being are jeopardized, fear is a likely concomitant emotional response. Should a counselor hear a client describing a situation where he broke or is considering breaking an especially significant moral or ethical code, the counselor might hypothesize that the client is experiencing feelings of guilt about that situation. Since a counselor's ability to respond to a client's emotions depends upon how accurately he infers the emotions, as an assessment about a client's feelings is an important counselor activity.

Self-concept   Another significant component of human functioning about which counselors frequently make assessments is the client's set of beliefs or attitudes toward himself—his self-concept or self-theory. Several important dimensions may be involved in discussing a client's beliefs about himself. First, are his beliefs favorable or unfavorable? Are they realistic or out of proportion to what might be realistically expected? To what degree are a person's ideals about himself discrepant or inconsistent with his beliefs about himself? What implications might this discrepancy have for the client's ability to function effectively? The basic model here is that a favorable change in a client's belief about himself may result in a favorable change in his ability to engage in a more rewarding behavior. For such a client, an appropriate counseling strategy might be to help him change his image of himself. This would influence other favorable changes to occur.

Interpersonal Relationship Characteristics A considerable proportion of human behavior is interpersonal behavior. Speech, for example, is behavior whose purpose is to communicate with others. Thus, one might reasonably expect that interpersonal relationships are frequently the root of the presenting problem for many clients. A variety of dimensions has been developed to describe interpersonal behaviors. One is related to trust vs. mistrust. Does the client demonstrate trust or does he arbitrarily distrust everyone (including the counselor)? Can he accurately discriminate between those for whom trust is appropriate and those for whom trust would result in undesirable consequences? Honesty vs. facade is another interpersonal dimension. Does he present himself honestly in his interpersonal relationships, or does he present a facade for the purpose of trying to make a certain kind of impression? Whether the client is outgoing or withdrawn is another interpersonal dimension. Of major importance is the relationship between certain emotions and interpersonal situations. Is the client generally tense in interpersonal situations or generally relaxed? What kinds of interpersonal situations are especially critical situations for him?

Client Expectations A significant factor concerning client functioning is the set of expectations he holds. Expectations are predictions concerning what will happen in certain situations. With some clients, certain expectations are inappropriate and unrealistic. A client's entering expectations concerning the counselor and the counseling process may be the difference between the success and failure of the counseling intervention. If so, an essential part of the counselor's strategy may be to deal with these entering expectations. Later, in the counseling process, an appropriate counseling strategy may be to help a client modify his expectations about certain important life situations. For example, a client who expects punishment from adults in general and who manifests strong fear in the presence of adults may be helped considerably by looking at those expectations and modifying them so that he learns that he may expect encouragement and support from some adults.

Personality Construct Dimensions   An infinite variety of personality construct dimensions may be invoked in the assessment of clients. One important construct is the dimension of "openness vs. closedness." Is the client guarded, defensive, resistant, or is he open, honest, and candid? How willing is he to be completely honest with himself as well as with the counselor?

A related dimension is that of repressor-sensitizer. Repressors are people who block from awareness potentially stressful or threatening ideas. At the other extreme, sensitizers are people who are extremely concerned about their perceived inadequacies, inabilities, etc. The rigid vs. flexible dimension refers to the degree to which a client is willing to look at alternatives. Clients whose behavior is described as rigid are those who have certain beliefs which are fixed and unalterable. Clients who are described as flexible are those who readily examine seriously alternative positions with which they are confronted. For some clients, with some kinds of counseling goals, assessment along these dimensions will influence the counselor's strategy. For other clients, the counselor's intervention strategy will be independent of such assessment.

For clients whose presenting problem has to do with making decisions about careers and education, an essential part of the counselor's role is to help them assess their skills, talents, abilities, and interests. This means helping the client describe himself with respect to his comparative strengths and weaknesses. With respect to his intellective functioning abilities, many tests, both group and individually administered, are available. Other tests, such as the

Differential Aptitude Test and the *General Aptitude Test Battery,* are available to assess more specific kinds of skills. (The latter is administered by the United States Employment Service.) Other tests are available to help client and counselor assess very specific skills, such as reading rate, reading comprehension, musical talent, etc. For a complete compendium of all such tests, the reader is referred to Buros, O. K., ed., *The Sixth Mental Measurements Yearbook* (Highland Park, N. J.: Gryphon Press, 1965). For readings on the use, application, and interpretation of tests, the reader should refer to works dealing with psychological testing, tests in counseling, personality measurement and assessment, and psychological measurement in general.

Client "interests" constitute another set of variables which are very much related to career and educational choices. Interest usually refers to the degree of preference a person demonstrates for certain kinds of activities. Some people prefer hiking through the woods to reading a book; for others, the preference is vice versa. Still others prefer building and constructing things with their hands to either of the above activities. Clearly, a person's preference for or interest in certain kinds of activities as opposed to other kinds of activities would appear to be related to the kinds of careers in which he would find enjoyment (assuming he has the talent to perform well in various job roles). *The Kuder Preference Tests* and the *Strong Vocational Interest Blank* are two available instruments to help client and counselor consider the client's comparative interests.

Level of aspiration is yet another dimension many counselors believe is important in helping clients consider decisions. Making reliable and valid assessments concerning this dimension can be difficult. Many high school seniors verbalize high levels of aspiration to significant adults in their lives, but once in college and away from home, they fail to act consistently with those stated levels of aspiration. Clients whose level of aspirations is out of proportion to their talents represent challenging cases to counselors. Both types of discrepancies are challenging. For the client who has much talent and little ambition, the counselor may feel a strong push to try to raise the client's level of aspiration. At times, this may represent a serious discrepancy in value judgments concerning what is in the client's best interest. At other times, this "inappropriately" low level of aspiration may reflect some serious client inhibitions. On the other hand, the counselor may see some clients with limited talent, but with an infinitely high level of aspiration, as people who will eventually encounter a series of devastating failure experiences.

Several essential points must be made about evaluation, assessment, and testing. The act of assessing is a behavior of the counselor, and like all other counselor behaviors, "assessing activities" are purposive and goal directed. With respect to involvement with his client, counselor assessment and diagnosis activity can be justified only if the counselor's in-counseling activities will in some way be influenced by the assessments and diagnoses he makes. In the past, many counselors and psychotherapists have engaged in the practice of "psychological voyeurism"—tests were administered, diagnoses, evaluations, and assessments made, and nothing happened afterwards. Assessment became a goal in and of itself. Insofar as the client is concerned, assessment is only a process goal to help in facilitating the achievement of outcome goals. If the counselor's in-counseling activities will not be influenced by the assessments he makes, he has no business making such assessments. The only exception to this rule is the use of tests and other assessment procedures to gather data for research projects. And in this realm, the research project must be carefully planned and designed prior to the use of such assessment procedures.

Many counselors believe that using tests has more undesirable than desirable consequences in the long run. They believe that taking information from a test influences the counselor in that he treats the client as a member of a category rather than as an individual. This "stereotypes" the client. For example, suppose a counselor was counseling with an adolescent boy and learned that his score on a highly respected test of intelligence was in the "well-below-average range," would the counselor react differently to him? If so, would the counselor's differential reaction be on the basis of his categorizing the client? Would that be in the client's best interests? Would such categorizing enhance or interfere with the counselor's effectiveness? The point these critics make is that it is extremely difficult to avoid categorizing an individual and making inferences and predictions about him once test data about him are obtained. Such a tendency violates the assumption of individuality and uniqueness which counselors believe is the essential and vital factor of their effectiveness.

Following the determination of client psycho-physical input, the counselor has the responsibility to map a strategy which would facilitate client growth and development toward the identified goal. Initially, this requires the counselor's consent and confidence that the identified goal is worthwhile for the client and that the goal is realistic and can be achieved. Three conditions must hold for this consent to occur.

First, the stated outcome goals must not be inconsistent with the counselor's professional ethics. A serious dilemma here might be exemplified by the client who comes to the counselor for help in finding ways to avoid being drafted into military service. Clearly, in order to make such a decision, the counselor must have a clear understanding of the ethics, values, and operating principles which guide his behavior and influence his decision.

Second, the counselor must be competent to help his client attain his goal. The dilemma for counselor trainees is clear. To help his client, the counselor must believe he is competent. Yet trainees, having had little counseling experience, have no basis from which to judge their competence.

Third, the strategy used to help clients must be consistent with the counselor's code of ethics. One can easily modify a client's compulsive hair-pulling behavior by shaving his head, but such would generally not be considered an ethical form of intervention.

If the help sought by the client is in the counselor's realm of competence and if there is no question of the counselor's professional, ethical, or personal position, then the counselor proceeds to map out a strategy for counseling intervention. If the help asked for by the client is beyond the counselor's competencies, the client must be told and another source of help found. This process of finding someone else is termed "referral." If no referral sources are available, or are not available at the time, it is the responsibility of the counselor to continue to work with the client, staying within the framework of those things that he can perform competently. If for some ethical or personal deliberations the counselor is not willing to give the client the assistance he seeks, the referral source is an alternative open to the counselor. Three other alternatives are possible:

1. The counselor may openly and candidly explain to the client why he is not willing to help, and allow the client to decide whether he wants to continue the process knowing how the counselor feels about the goal.

2. A secondary goal may be established that can become the focus of the counseling process.

3. The counselor may attempt to persuade the client to consider another outcome goal which would be consistent with the counselor's sense of ethics.

As has been mentioned, a referral is the process of finding someone else to help the client. As conditions currently stand, referral may be more easily accomplished in some areas of the country than others. One factor is the unavailability of referral sources; that is, there may be no one available at the time to whom the counselor can send the client. Secondly, though there may be a referral source, the counselor may feel there is no one more competent than he, regardless of the referral source's job title or function. In any case, it is the responsibility of the counselor to continue to see the client, if that is the desire of the client. Under these circumstances, the best may be for the counselor to continue to maintain the relationship that has been established, and, by this relationship, provide the client with an opportunity for self-exploration and support.

In suggesting a referral, the counselor may leave it up to the client to make his own contact with the referral source, or he may make the initial contact for the client, with the client's permission and understanding. Some follow-up procedure is necessary, either with the referral source or the client, in order to determine if the counselor's further assistance is necessary in any capacity. Additional material on referrals and follow-up will be discussed later.

COUNSELING STRATEGIES   The term "strategy" is used to refer to the *planning process* of counseling. This process refers to the planning activity of the counselor in which he considers the goals of counseling and the characteristics of the client, and then systematically thinks through the process goals which must be attained if outcome goals are to be achieved. This includes the counselor thinking through how he will behave with his client so as to attain these goals. This is not meant to imply that the counselor's verbal responses to the client should be planned in advance to the last detail. Nor is it suggested that the sequence of what happens in face-to-face counseling must be rigidly controlled. Nevertheless, the general trend of what happens in the counseling situation and how it proceeds are the responsibility of the counselor. Within that rubric there is clearly plenty of room for flexibility and spontaneity.

Thus, there are several *action-related* questions which counselors must ask themselves: "How am I to proceed so as to have the greatest chance in achieving the outcome goals we have mutually agreed upon?" "What strategies, or courses of action, are most likely to result in the attainment of these outcome goals?" "What actions on my part might interfere in attaining these goals?" "Is there a sequence of things which must first occur (process goals) if counseling is to be successful?" "If so, can I clearly describe these process goals, which are necessary and instrumental, in attaining outcome goals?"

Since the attainment of counseling goals is directly related to the way the counselor behaves in the presence of his client, these questions clearly demand that the counselor focus on his own in-counseling behavior, especially, although not exclusively, his verbal behavior—what he *says to* the client. The key question is, "What sort of counselor behaviors will have what kind of *impact,* on which kind of clients, at what stage in the counseling process?" A counselor's skill is directly related to:

1. His ability to accurately *anticipate* the kind of impact he wants to have on his client.
2. His ability to behave in such ways as to have the intended impact.

The state of professional knowledge in the behavior intervention disciplines is a very long way from specifying the answers to questions a client may have about specific concerns. However, the mandates and responsibilities of counselors still remain. Further, there are some general process goals which may be considered relevant and appropriate for many clients with certain varieties of concerns. There are also certain kinds of strategies which appear potentially more effective for certain client concerns. In Chapter 6, several traditional counseling strategies and the model of human behavior, upon which these are based, will be examined.

CLIENT EDUCATION TO COUNSELING PROCEDURES There are times in the counseling process when it is desirable and/or necessary to educate the client to the counseling procedures that will be used to facilitate client growth toward the desired objective. It may be necessary that the client be aware of the procedure, the reasons why the counselor has decided to select such a procedure, how the client will feel during the procedural process, what it means for the client to reach his desired objective, and whether it will facilitate growth. Explanations, demonstrations, reading materials, are all appropriate forms of client education. At specific times, however, it is not desirable to educate the client to the procedures to be used, for example, if the counselor has decided to verbally reinforce the client expressions of more positive self-report. The procedures and treatments will be discussed later.

CLIENT COMMITMENT TO STRATEGY At this point, with the understanding the counselor has of the client, client input, and client-desired objective for counseling, along with counselor agreement and assessment of these factors, it is necessary for the counselor to help the client commit himself to the assistance offered in facilitating growth toward the desired goal. Most clients, as has been established, have several areas or matters in which they seek assistance. Out of the process stage of goal identification, the counselor helps the client to isolate, or at least identify, the one area in which he desires to be helped. The client must commit himself, verbally, to working in this area. The focus is in one area, in which some specific help can be given, rather than on a broad approach. This client commitment may be termed a verbal "contract."

THE CRITERIA FOR ASSESSING A SUCCESSFUL THIRD STAGE In order for the counselor to assess his success in helping the client to identify a goal of counseling, and to establish effective counseling strategies, the following criteria are offered, in question form:

1. Did I help the client to speak in a specific manner by:
   a. defining the terms he used?
   b. relating to specific historical events?
   c. taking a look at any physiological reaction he may have experienced at the time of the specific event?
   d. helping him to compare and contrast his behavior in various settings and under different circumstances?
2. Did I help the client to state a goal for his counseling experience?
3. Was this goal stated in behavioral terms?
4. Am I sure the client has no physical incapacity or disability which might hinder his development toward the goal? If there were some questions, did I proceed in an appropriate manner as described?
5. Do I have data, gathered through psychological assessment, that are necessary and dependent upon the client's stated goal?
6. Do I believe the client's goal is realistic and achievable? If not, did I follow an appropriate course of action?
7. Limited by my competencies, can I help the client toward his goal or must I take another course of action, such as referral, or must I simply maintain the facilitative relationship? If not, did I follow an appropriate course of action?
8. Do I feel ethically and personally that I can and want to help the client reach his goal? If not, did I follow an appropriate course of action?
9. Is the strategy I have chosen proper and within my realm of competencies?
10. Does the client understand (if appropriate) what I am going to do to help him?
11. Is the client committed toward accepting my stated assistance in facilitating growth toward his desired goal?

SUMMARY

The ultimate goal of this third stage in the counseling process is the preparation of the counselor and client for the next stage in the counseling process. The client, with the counselor's aid, has determined the goal for counseling. The counselor has assessed the physical and psychological characteristics the client brings to the counseling process which are related to attaining the goals of counseling. The counselor has consented to help the client, and has mapped out a strategy for such help. The client has been prepared for the procedures to be used and has made a verbal contract in this regard. This stage having been satisfactorily completed, and, while maintaining the facilitative relationship, the counselor and client are ready to move into the next stage of the counseling process.

CASE OF ALLISON   Allison is twenty-five years of age and the mother of three small children. This typescript is taken from the last few minutes of the third session. The client has previously discussed her "lack of confidence," has defined this term, and has indicated events and situations in which she feels this way.

Counselor 1:   Last week you mentioned that you wanted your husband to have counseling and that you didn't see where you felt counseling was helping you in your marriage and this is something I wanted to point out to you. This is true. Possibly your husband needs counseling and what we are doing now is not marriage counseling.

Client 1:   No; that's right.

Counselor 2:   What I would like for you to do now is to think about what you want to accomplish.

Comments: The purpose of Counselor 2 is to clearly identify the goals of counseling more specifically. With so many non-specific goals, the counselor cannot focus his efforts toward any one goal. Note that at Counselor 3, the counselor effectively follows up in pursuit of that process goal.

Client 2:   Here?

Counselor 3:   Right. And where I can help you, okay? Think about the thing that you want to start with most. Can you tell me now what you want to start with most?

Client 3:   The thing I want to start with most is . . . . The first thing that comes to mind just when you said it without any real forethought is oh, I would like to develop a confidence in myself that I don't have, whether I appear to anybody that wanders around and looks at me to have it but I know I do but I don't feel it really, but I feel a little more really since I have been talking to you. . . . I don't know why, but I do. But this ridiculous thing about never wanting to offend people which is absurd; you can't go through life like that. Buckling under when I don't really want to, which I have always done —it irritates me when I do it. That is something I would like to try and I'll give you a start—a good example of something that makes me very angry with myself that I just don't drive, I want to drive, I would like to drive, but I don't particular want the responsibility—scares me to death, having all my children, with me like, all the time in that car and having all that power under me and all that power around me and really the ability to murder someone if you aren't on your toes all the time, and I don't want to do it because I don't feel capable of doing a good job because I'm not particularly coordinated. . . . It scares me to death, but I want to drive.

Counselor 4:   Go home and think about it; use this

week to think about it, the thing that is most important that you want to accomplish here.

Comments: Should the counselor have responded to some of the themes in the client's remark at Client 3? Lack of self-confidence, inability to be assertive in interpersonal situations, and fear of killing someone are three themes the client has communicated. Might there have been a good reason why the counselor chose not to respond to any of these?

Client 4:   With me.

Counselor 5:   Right.

Client 5:   Oh gee; all right, I'll think about that. There are so many—not necessary minor, but so many things I would like to change with me.

Counselor 6:   Think what you want to work on first, something that is really important and you want to work on first.

Client 7:   Okay. You are giving me a point [*Laughs*]. Direction—now I don't get to sit and babble anymore. I don't know if anyone is really totally satisfied with themselves. Thanks.

SUGGESTIONS FOR
FURTHER READING

Bandura, A.
　1961　"Psychotherapy as a Learning Process." *Psychological Bulletin,* 58:143–159.
　1969　*Principles of Behavior Modification.* New York: Holt, Rinehart and Winston.

Ellis, A.
　1967　"Goals of Psychotherapy." In A. H. Mahrer, ed. *The Goals of Psychotherapy.* New York: Appleton-Century-Crofts.

Goldman, L.
　1961　*Using Tests in Counseling.* New York: Appleton-Century-Crofts.
　1964　"The Process of Vocational Assessment." In H. Borow, ed. *Man in a World at Work.* Boston: Houghton Mifflin.

Hosford, R.
　1969　"Behavioral Counseling: A Contemporary Overview." *The Counseling Psychologist,* 4:1–33.

Krumboltz, J. D.
　1965　"Behavioral Counseling: Rationale and Research." *Personnel and Guidance Journal,* 44:383–387.
　1966　"Behavioral Goals for Counseling." *Journal of Counseling Psychology,* 13:153–159.

Mager, R. F.
　1962　*Preparing Instructional Objectives.* Palo Alto, Calif.: Fearon Press.

Mahrer, A.
　1968　*The Goals of Psychotherapy.* New York: Appleton-Century-Crofts.

Peterson, D. L.
　1968　*The Clinical Study of Social Behavior.* New York: Appleton-Century-Crofts.

Ryan, T. A.
　1969　"Systems Techniques for Programs of Counseling and Counselor Education." *Educational Technology,* 9:7–17.

Thoresen, C. E.
　1969　"The Systems Approach and Counselor Education: Basic Features and Implications." *Counselor Education and Supervision,* 9:3–17.

Ullmann, L. and Krasner, L.
　1965　*Case Studies in Behavior Modification.* New York: Holt, Rinehart and Winston.

Chapter 6   Counseling Strategies

This chapter will consider the various strategies available to the counselor to help him achieve the kind of change he and his client have agreed upon as desirable. Since strategies for change are based upon principles of human behavior acquisition, the approach will be to articulate some of these basic principles and then to describe the kinds of strategies based upon these principles. The format for this chapter, then, is to describe those principles of behavior development which apply to the counseling process.

The counselor's *impact* is directly related to his ability to systematically apply these principles in the counseling situation.

The concept "strategy" refers to the counselor activity of planning in advance how to apply such principles systematically, and then to implement the plan so as to achieve maximum desired impact. A counselor's impact is directly related to his behavior in the presence of clients, and his behavior is directly related to the systematic application of the principles of change, some of which will be described in this chapter.

Before developing these principles, it is crucial to emphasize that the *timing* and sequence of application are factors which are vital to the successful application of these principles. Premature application may result in disastrous impact. These principles can be applied productively only after an effective relationship has been attained and the goals of counseling have been clearly described.

PRINCIPLES AND STRATEGIES NOT BASED ON AWARENESS AS A PROCESS GOAL

Principle 1—People Learn New Behaviors by Receiving Verbal Instructions From Significant Others   Some obvious examples of this principle would include parents teaching their children which behaviors are appropriate and which are inappropriate at home, and a sports professional teaching a novice to execute the skills of a sport. This is also the model upon which most classroom activities are based. Students allegedly learn by being verbally instructed by the significant other labelled "teacher." Such instruction includes (a) explaining, making clear or intelligent, (b) expounding, stating, or setting forth the meaning of something, and (c) simple instruction, imparting knowledge, directions, and commands.

This would suggest that one potential counselor change strategy would be to verbally instruct the client as to what behaviors are appropriate and how the client can execute such behaviors. A word of caution: There are some serious secondary consequences in implementing such a strategy. In actual counselor behavior, this strategy generally takes the form of advice giving: "You should do this. . . ." or "You should do it this way. . . ." Such advice giving may be maladaptive in the sense that it may actually interfere with the attainment of counseling outcome goals. If the advice is given too early, it may be inappropriate. If the client acts on the advice and it is inappropriate, his subsequent action will be inappropriate.

In such a case, the counselor would be responsible for influencing the client to act in ways which are actually contrary to his best interest.

If the client rejects the advice given, he may, in the act of doing so, come to the conclusion that the person who gave the inappropriate advice is not a viable source of help. *He has rejected the counselor as a helping person.* Even if he does not, the relationship may be seriously jeopardized. Further, especially with many adolescents in school situations, what they feel they need *least* is another adult in their environment telling them what to do. Adolescents in school will tend to reject advice even if they ask for it, and In so doing, they will reject the advice giver as a source of help. Finally, most people who write on the goals of education see the act of helping students learn to behave "independently" as an important educational goal ("independently" here means deciding for oneself what is appropriate action and then acting on the basis of that decision). Offering advice is clearly inconsistent with "independence" as an educational goal. Paradoxically, then, advice giving as an appropriate intervention strategy for counselors is not advised. Advice giving is especially maladaptive when it is given too early in the counseling process; that is, when it is given before a strong relationship has been established. Special note of this advice-giving tendency is made because clients frequently ask the counselor for advice, and in so doing, the counselor frequently is seduced into giving advice. This is especially true of counselors in the early stages of their professional training.

The techniques included in the instructional approach to counseling procedures have as their goal the learning by the client of new or different ways of behaving in specific circumstances. This learning is the result of the counselor instructing, teaching, telling by explaining, expounding, directing, or interpreting. The following techniques will be reviewed:

1. Systematic desensitization
    a. Training in progressive relaxation
    b. Desensitization proper
2. Paradoxical intention (anti-suggestion)
3. Direct instruction
4. Bibliotherapy

5. Thought interference
6. Assertive training
7. Aversion training

Systematic Desensitization An important treatment approach which has developed from the behavior modification literature is called "systematic desensitization." The system is generally used to reduce or eliminate undesirable and maladaptive anxiety responses and to replace these responses with relaxation responses which are considered to be incompatible with the anxiety responses. The rationale is that anxiety responses are elicited (or triggered) by certain stimulus conditions. The development of this stimulus-response connection can be accounted for by principles of conditioning. Once conditioned, the individual is largely unable to control the occurrence of the anxiety responses when he is faced with the particular stimulus condition. The anxiety responses are noxious and interfere with the person's attempts to cope more effectively with the situation. Technically, a person experiencing such difficulties is said to have developed a phobia. Further, consistent with the principle of generalization, situations which are similar to the phobic situation may also elicit anxiety responses, although not as severe in intensity. People experiencing such a phobia can usually rank order stimulus conditions on the basis of the intensity of the anxiety they elicit. This is crucial observation, for the elimination of a phobia depends on utilizing this generalization principle.

Using systematic desensitization to reduce a phobia involves three basic stages: establishing a response hierarchy (or list which rank orders the stimulus conditions on the basis of the intensity of anxiety each elicits); training the person to become very deeply relaxed; and having him imagine himself in each of the situations on the hierarchy while he is in a state of deep relaxation. Short of using drugs (which frequently have undesirable side effects), the most powerful method for helping people become relaxed is the method known as deep muscle relaxation. Using this procedure, clients are trained to tense certain muscle groups and then suddenly relax them. By carefully controlling the intensity and duration of tension, and carefully programming the sequence of muscle groups, the counselor can usually train his client to become more deeply relaxed than he has ever been before. Deep relaxation is incompatible with anxiety; the two are mutually exclusive responses. If relaxation responses can be conditioned to occur under certain stimulus conditions, they will prevent or inhibit the occurrence of anxiety responses in those same situations.

Based on the principle of stimulus generalization, the counselor systematically conditions relaxation to occur instead of anxiety. After training the client to achieve a state of deep relaxation, he tells the client to imagine himself in each of the situations on the hierarchy. By carefully controlling the duration in which each of the images is flashed, and the sequence in which they are flashed, the counselor has a powerful method of replacing anxiety responses with relaxation responses. He begins with short flashes of the entry on the hierarchy which elicits least anxiety. After progressing to longer durations of that image, he proceeds to the next image on the hierarchy, and again controls the imagining of that entry. When the client no longer reports anxiety after a number of trials of that image, the counselor proceeds to the next step in the hierarchy, and goes through the same process. In this fashion, he proceeds through each entry in the hierarchy beginning with the one which elicits least anxiety, and then proceeds to the next step in the hierarchy. Thus, by the time the situations high in the hierarchy are reached, the intensity of anxiety responses to these situations has already been reduced.

Training in Progressive Relaxation   It should be explained to the subject that this is the most important procedure in the treatment and, therefore, must be mastered if counseling is to have any chance of being successful. The following is the method:

The client should be seated in an overstuffed chair. Legs should be extended, head resting on the back of the chair, and arms resting on the arms of the chair. No part of the body should require the use of muscles for support. The room should be quiet and the lights dimmed. The subject should then be put through relaxation exercises. The instructions follow:

> Hold the arm of the chair quite tightly. I want you to observe certain things that are a result of your holding this chair tightly. First of all, there are certain sensa-

tions. To begin with, you have sensations in your hand; you may experience other sensations. With your right hand, point out to me all the places where you get any kind of feeling which seems to be the result of holding the chair tightly. Now, let go of the chair and notice the different feeling entering the relaxing muscles. We are now going to go through most of your body. As you tense and relax each of these muscles, focusing on the sensations, you will begin to learn the difference between a state of tension and a state of complete relaxation. As you learn this, you will become deeply relaxed, more deeply relaxed than you have ever been before.

Now, I want you to make a fist with your right hand, tensing the muscles of your right hand and forearm; tense, until it trembles. Feel the muscles pull across your fingers and the lower part of your forearm (hold the fist tightly for five to seven seconds). Now, just release your fist and relax. Pay attention to the muscles of your right hand and forearm as they relax. Note how those muscles feel as relaxation flows through them. (Relaxation period should last from ten to twenty seconds.)

Again tense the muscles of your right hand and forearm. Pay attention to the muscles involved. Notice how the muscles pull across the top of the hand in the fingers and in the upper and lower part of the forearm. Now, let the hand go limp. Feel how the relaxation flows over the hand and forearm. Your hand and forearm are becoming deeply relaxed, more deeply relaxed than ever before. Each time we do this, you'll relax even more until your arm and hand are completely relaxed with no tension at all, warm and relaxed.

(Instruct the client to raise a finger if his right hand and forearm are completely relaxed—this usually takes from two to four tries.)

Using the same procedure, have the subject tense his right biceps, leaving his hand and forearm on the chair. Proceed in the same manner as above, in a hypnotic monotone, using the (right) hand as a reference point. For example, move on when the client reports his right biceps feels as completely relaxed as his right hand and forearm.

The following are statements which can be used to put the client into a relaxed state:

1. You are feeling sensations of numbness or tingling.
2. You are experiencing the effortless, pleasant feelings of relaxation.
3. Release the muscles and feel how the relaxation flows in.
4. Feel the sensations of warmth and relaxation.
5. Just let yourself sink deeper and heavier into the chair . . . heavier . . . and deeper.
6. A pleasant feeling of warmth and heaviness is entering your body as you become more and more deeply relaxed . . . more comfortably relaxed.
7. Growing deeper and still deeper, somehow getting even heavier . . . and more relaxed.
8. Each time you exhale you are getting more relaxed . . . more and more relaxed, deeply relaxed.
9. You are letting your muscles go further and further into relaxation; they are becoming more loose . . . loose and heavy, and relaxed.
10. Your breathing is becoming easier and more rhythmical— no energy is being used.
11. Your body is feeling very heavy and calm.
12. Just breathe right out, relaxing and enjoying the soothing relief; all the muscles of your body are becoming more relaxed every time you exhale. Go on breathing normally, easily, freely, completely relaxed.
13. Continue relaxing for awhile, enjoying the calm, pleasant sensation of deep, total relaxation; your hands and arms are limp, your shoulders resting naturally, your face and neck muscles relaxed and serene.
14. Breathe deeply, in and out, in and out.
15. The tensions are vanishing from your forehead.
16. You are letting the muscles of your _____ continue relaxing until they are as relaxed as the muscles of your _____.

17. You can feel how it is to be completely relaxed.
18. You can tell the difference between a state of tenseness and a state of complete relaxation.

Having relaxed the right dominant hand, forearm, and biceps, the counselor should proceed to other gross-muscle groups in the same manner.

1. For the non-dominant (left) hand and forearm: You can feel the muscles and skin of your left hand pulling over the knuckles.
2. For the non-dominant (left) biceps, proceed as in step 1.
3. For the muscles of forehead and top of the face: Frown hard, tensing the muscles of forehead and top of the face. Relax. You can feel the tensions vanishing from your forehead.
4. Squinch your eyes tightly and wrinkle up your nose. Tighter, tighter—you can notice the tension around your eyes and nose; now—relax—you are letting all the muscles around your eyes and nose completely relax and the relaxation spreads over your entire face. You can observe the difference between tension and complete relaxation as you let your muscles become completely and deeply relaxed.
5. Draw the corners of your mouth back, feeling the jaw and cheek muscles pull, and noticing the tension in your cheek and jaw muscles.
6. Push your head forward pressing your chin against your chest, feeling the muscles in your neck pull.
7. Pull your shoulders back, feeling the muscles become tighter in your chest and back.
8. Pull your stomach in and try to push it against your backbone. Feel the muscles tighten.
9. Push your stomach out making the muscles tighter, as if you expect someone to punch you in the stomach.
10. Tighten muscles of your right upper leg—feel one muscle on top and two muscles on the bottom of the upper leg tighten.
11. Push your toes forward, arching your right foot, keeping your heel on the floor. You can feel the muscles tighten in the under portion of your right calf. Feel the pressure as if something were pushing up under the arch.

12. Keeping your heel on the floor, pull your foot back feeling the muscles in the upper portion of your calf pull tightly.

13. Left upper leg.

14. Left under-portion of the calf.

15. Left upper-portion of the calf.

For most muscle groups, it will only be necessary to tense and relax the muscle twice. However, for certain stubborn muscle groups, it may be necessary to go through the tension-release process three or four times in order to reach an optimal state of relaxation. Many clients find the tension-release cycle more effective when they inhale deeply and hold their breath while tensing muscles, and then exhale while releasing the muscles. When a muscle group does not respond after four trials, move on and return to it later. It must be remembered that some subjects might develop muscle cramps from prolonged tensing of the muscles. If this occurs, cut a few seconds off the tensing period and instruct the client not to tense the muscles quite so hard.

Clients will be brought back to "normal" by means of the numerical method of trance termination: "I am going to count from one to four. On the count of one, start moving your legs; two, your fingers and hands; three, your head; and four, open your eyes and sit up. One, move your legs; two, now your fingers and hands; three, move your head around; four, open your eyes and sit up." The counselor should not allow the subject to leave the chair until it appears that he has returned to a relatively normal state. All subjects will be asked if they feel alert before they leave.

All clients will be asked to try to practice twice a day for not more than fifteen minutes each time. These practice sessions should be at least three hours apart. The practice sessions should be held when the subject is alone. It should be suggested to each client that his second practice session could be accomplished while lying in bed at night just before going to sleep.

By the third session, if the client has been practicing relatively well, relaxation can be induced by a modified relaxation period method as follows:

1. Stretch out both arms, making a tighter and tighter fist. Now relax.

2. Face (same as original method).

3. Neck (same as original method).

4. Chest (same as original method).

5. Stomach (same as original method).

6. Stretch out both legs pointing your toes outward and tense up all the muscles in your legs. Make the muscles tighter and tighter. Now, relax.

Desensitization proper   This technique or procedure is used together with training in progressive relaxation to help a client overcome a fear or phobia such as, height, water, closed spaces, elevators, darkness, etc. The client is first trained in progressive relaxation, and then, with an established hierarchy of anxiety-producing stimuli, is desensitized, systematically, to these stimuli.

The hierarchy may be a series of statements that help the client recall an experience, photos or other pictures that may be used to help recall, or the actual stimuli, if this is feasible. The following explanations may be given the client:

1. Procedure: The specific technique we will be using is called desensitization. This method of treatment is based on the picturing of situations in your mind while you are completely relaxed. You will find yourself more relaxed than you have ever been before. In case you are wondering if my objective is hypnosis, it is not. At no time during this treatment will you be hypnotized. You will simply be in a state of very deep relaxation, which you should find very comfortable. Relaxation alone can be used to reduce tension. However, the ability to relax completely will take time for you to acquire. Therefore, it will be necessary for you to practice the technique of relaxation between our sessions.

2. Construction of anxiety hierarchy: There are probably certain situations in which you find yourself becoming more tense than others. I have here a set of cards, each of which has a situation described on it. I would like you to arrange these cards so that the situation in which you feel most comfortable comes first, followed by those situations in which you feel less and less comfortable. The last card in your arrangement should contain the situation in which you feel the most uncomfortable.

The client's imagery should be tested as soon as he has been relaxed in the second session as follows:

"I would like to test your ability to visualize objects. With your eyes closed try to visualize yourself lying in bed in your room just before going to sleep. Can you see it? Try to describe what you are now imagining in your mind. Okay, erase that image and continue relaxing." The subject's visualization should at least be as clear as a vivid memory. With practice, images should become clearer. The subject should be made to realize that he should visualize the situations as if he were there—not simply watching himself.

Next, the client should be told that he is going to begin working on the items on the tension scale and that he will be asked to picture these items in his mind, the easiest situation on the tension scale first. He should also be told that if at any time he begins to feel uneasy or tense, he should signal by raising his right forefinger. If either the client signals anxiety, or the counselor notices that the client is tensing up, the client should be instructed to immediately erase the image from his mind and continue relaxing. The client should then be asked in which muscles he felt tension. The counselor should then instruct the subject to tense and relax these muscle groups and to continue to relax until he is back to a pre-anxiety state of complete relaxation. The counselor should then go back one step in the hierarchy. If no anxiety has been evoked by the presentation of this item, the counselor returns to the previous anxiety-evoking item, having the client visualize it now for only three to five seconds. If no anxiety is felt during this brief presentation, the counselor proceeds to work through that item, and then introduces the next item on the hierarchy. Any time anxiety is felt, the same procedure should be followed. However, whenever anxiety to the same item is signaled more than once in a single session, the client should be asked if there was less tension present the second time. In addition, sometimes the steps in the anxiety hierarchy may be too great. When this is the case, interpolation of new items between steps may be necessary.

The general procedure should be as follows: Each item should be presented three consecutive times unless anxiety is present. Each item should be visualized for five seconds. If no anxiety has been signaled, thirty to forty-five seconds should be allowed to elapse before the item is presented a second time, for ten seconds. If no anxiety has been signaled, twenty seconds should be allowed to elapse before the item is presented a third time, for fifteen seconds. As each item is completed in this manner, attention is placed on the next item in the hierarchy.

The first item in the hierarchy should be made very easy so that the client can gain experience with the procedure. For example, the client becomes experienced when he can picture scenes when deeply relaxed and then be able to switch them off when no anxiety is present.

The counselor must possess good clinical sensitivity if the treatment is to be successful, for he must know when to go back, when to construct new items, and when to move up the hierarchy.

At the beginning of each session, the subject should be reminded about the importance of visualizing the scenes as vividly as possible. Reminders to signal anxiety should also be stressed. Every session should begin with the next to the last item that has been successfully completed in a previous session. Every session should be ended with the presentation of an item which has not evoked any anxiety. Most clients should be able to go through the entire hierarchy in five sessions.

The following is a demonstration of the use of systematic desensitization in the treatment of a phobic reaction—flying as a passenger in an airplane. This is a segment from the fourth session in the use of this strategy, the seventh session in the counseling process.

Counselor: You're completely relaxed, at ease. There's no tension anywhere in your body. Your arms, your legs, completely sinking down into the couch. Now, I would like to test your ability to visualize objects with your eyes closed; try to visualize yourself in a pleasant situation. Visualize the situation as if you were there—not simply watching yourself. Do you have a mental picture? All right, try to describe to me what you are now imagining in your mind.

Client: [*Client describes a scene at home with her husband. Due to her state of relaxation her voice is too faint to be picked up on the tape.*]

Counselor: All right, fine, erase that scene from your mind. Now, we are going to begin working on the items in your tension scale. I'm going to request that you picture certain situations in your mind. If at anytime you begin to feel uneasy or tense, I would like you to signal by raising your right forefinger about an inch.

Now I want you to imagine that you are in your home. It's very cool and comfortable and you are seated near the telephone. [*Pause*] All right, stop imagining this scene. Now, if that scene didn't worry you, if you felt nothing, don't do anything. If that scene disturbed you, raise your right finger. All right, just keep on relaxing.

Now, I want you to imagine that you're seated at the telephone—and you're talking to the airline's clerk and you're making a reservation for an airplane trip. [*Pause*] Now, stop imagining that. Now, if imagining that disturbed you even a very small bit, I want you to raise your right index finger. If it didn't worry you, do nothing.

Now once again, I want you to imagine that you're seated at the telephone, you're talking to the airline's clerk, you're making reservations for an air trip. [*Pause*] All right, stop imagining that. If you felt any disturbance, raise your right index finger; all right, just keep on relaxing. Concentrate on your muscles. Sink deeply into the couch—very, very relaxed.

Now, I want you to imagine yourself in front of the airlines office. You enter, you walk to the counter, then you purchase a ticket. [*Pause*] Now, stop imagining that. Now, if imagining that disturbed you even a small bit, I want you to raise your right index finger. If you felt nothing, do nothing. Fine, concentrate on your muscles. Sink deeply into your calm, relaxed state.

Now, I want you to imagine that you're in an automobile. You're approaching the air terminal, the car stops in front, you get out, and you walk into the terminal. [*Pause*] All right, erase that image from your mind. If the image that you saw disturbed you, raise your right index finger. Fine, just keep on relaxing.

Once more, imagine that you're in an automobile. You're approaching the air terminal, you stop in front, get out, you walk into the terminal. [*Pause*] All right, erase that from your mind. If you felt any disturbance, raise your right index finger.

Imagine, once more, you're in an automobile. You look out and you see the air terminal. The car stops in front, you get out, and you walk into the building. [*Pause*] All right, now, stop imagining that. Just relax. Concentrate on your muscles. If you felt any disturbance, raise your right index finger. Very well.

Now, I would like you to imagine that you are following a redcap who is carrying your luggage. You walk up to the check-in counter, you check in your luggage. [*Pause*] Now, stop imagining that. Now, if imagining that disturbed you even the smallest amount, I want you to raise your right index finger. If it didn't, do nothing.

Now, once again, I want you to imagine that you are following a redcap who's carrying your luggage. You walk up to the counter, your luggage is weighed in, you talk with the clerk, she examines your ticket. [*Pause*] All right, stop imagining that. If you felt any disturbance, any tension, I would like you to raise your right index finger. All right, continue relaxing. You're experiencing a state of complete relaxation, there's no tension in your body. You feel very calm, very relaxed.

All right, imagine that you're sitting in the terminal, you're waiting. You look out of the window and you see planes departing. [*Pause*] Now, stop imagining that. If you felt disturbed, even a small amount, I want you to raise your right index finger. If it didn't worry you, do nothing.

Once again, you're sitting in the waiting room, you're waiting for a plane. You look out of the window and you see planes departing. [*Pause*] Now, erase that image from your mind. Continue relaxing. If you felt any disturbance, any tension, raise your right index finger. All right, just keep on relaxing. Concentrate on your muscles.

Now, I want you to picture that you're walking through the terminal towards the boarding gate. You arrive at the gate, you have your ticket checked. [*Pause*] Now, stop imagining that. If that image disturbed you, even a small bit, I want you to raise your right index finger. Just relax. In what muscles did you feel ten sion?

Client: My head.

Counselor: All right, squinch up the muscles of youɪ forehead, and your eyes.

Client: I mean inside of my brain

Counselor: Oh, sorry.

Client: I'm relaxed—now.

Counselor: Relax all of the muscles of your body. Feel the relaxation flow through. Your arms are limp, your legs, very relaxed. Sink right down into the couch.

Now, once again, I want you to imagine that you're walking through the terminal towards the boarding gate. You arrive at the gate, take out your ticket, and have your ticket checked. [*Pause*] Now, stop imagining that. If imagining that disturbed you, raise your right index finger. Concentrate on your muscles, just keep on relaxing.

Now, once again, you get up from the seat, walk through the terminal towards the boarding gate. You arrive at the gate, there's a cluster of people standing around, you wait your turn. Then you have your ticket checked. [*Pause*] Now, stop imagining that. If you felt any disturbance at all, even the smallest amount, I want you to raise your right index finger. All right, relax. There's no tension in your body—completely relaxed.

Imagine that you're in the waiting room, you're sitting there, you're reading the newspaper, you glance out of the window, and you see planes. [*Pause*] All right, stop imagining that. If that scene disturbed you even a small amount, I want you to raise your right index finger. Very good, continue to relax. Concentrate on your muscles.

I would like you to imagine that you're sitting in the waiting room. You look out of the window and you see planes. There are many planes, they're landing, they're taxiing towards the building. You look into the distance and you see another plane coming in. [*Pause*] All right, stop imagining that. If you felt any tension imagining that scene, raise your right index finger. Fine, keep on relaxing. Sink right down into the couch. You're completely at ease, no tension anywhere in your body.

All right, now imagine that you're sitting in the waiting room. You get up, you walk down the corridor towards the boarding gate. [*Pause*] Now, stop imagining that. If you felt any disturbance at all, even a small bit, I want you to raise your right index finger. All right, relax. Concentrate on your muscles. There's no tension in your body—the muscles of your legs and your arms—limp, relaxed. Completely at ease.

Paradoxical Intention (Anti-suggestion) This technique is based on the assumption that fear makes what is feared come true, and that positively portraying the symptoms of fear makes what is feared appear ridiculous. For example, if a client is frightened by an object or circumstance, the more she tries not to be frightened, the more fearful she will become. On the other hand, if she consciously attempts to be frightened and feels the symptoms of fear, she will feel less fearful.

Three successful case procedures are presented. All three are taken from actual counseling records:

Case one. Bill, age twenty-seven, was afraid of having a heart attack. Although physical examinations, including electrocardiograms, revealed no evidence of heart disease, the client was still troubled by tightness and occasional sharp pains in his chest. The goal of counseling was to eliminate the fear of a coronary by the method of paradoxical intention. The purpose of this method was to enable the client to develop a sense of detachment toward his fear by replacing the fear with a paradoxical desire: "My heart is going to beat faster and faster, then stop, and I'll die right here."

The client was encouraged to place himself in the situations described during the goal identification stage and to help himself by the use of this technique.

Case two. Miss Jones had an intense fear of riding in elevators. Her employer moved his offices to the top floor in an office building thereby making it necessary for the client to ride an elevator. The goal of counseling was to help Miss Jones eliminate her fear of elevators.

The counselor instructed the client to visualize entering an elevator and to demonstrate her fear, in an attempt to detach the client from the fear. Such instructions as, "Show some real terror now!" "Come on now, panic, and run around the room!" evoked humor and helped remove the client from her fear. Miss Jones was urged to continue practicing this technique in real situations.

Case three. A young woman was afraid of burglars while in the house alone. The client was basically well adjusted and had very little real grounds on which to base her fear. She was instructed to portray her fear while in the counseling situation. Humor was evoked by the counselor's instructions to "shake, stutter, perspire, etc." Through repeated attempts, she was not able to demonstrate fear. She was asked to use this technique on herself when she was left alone in the house.

Direct Instruction   This procedure is used to help a client think (and, therefore, behave) in a more reasonable and rational manner. Sometimes fears about oneself can be attacked directly, and the faulty, unreasonable logic attached to the fears is exposed. The technique of direct instruction attacks these "fears about self," exposes them for the nonsense they are, and replaces them with sound logical thought processes. The following successful cases are illustrative of this procedure.

Case four. The client identified a fear of blushing as her main problem. This fear had bothered her considerably in the college classroom, her classroom as a teacher, in social gatherings, and in surprise situations, such as an unexpected meeting with a friend she had not seen for some time. Because of the fear of blushing and the consequent embarrassment, she had a good deal of difficulty behaving appropriately in these situations. She spoke of blushing as, "awful," "terrible," and "humiliating."

The client was instructed in the manner in which she was to maintain the disturbance by thinking of blushing as something awful, terrible, and humiliating. The counselor helped the client change her thinking about blushing to a point where she could accept it. This was done through the use of logic, reason, teaching, and suggestions. Her fear was reduced, she behaved more effectively in situations, and the instances of blushing were drastically reduced.

Case five. George, a high school senior, came to the counseling center because of difficulty he was having accepting himself as a person of average intelligence and achievement. His parents were disappointed with him because he had not been admitted to any of several premedical college programs to which he had applied. The client spoke of himself as a failure and an ungrateful son. These thoughts were taking most of his time and energy.

The counselor attempted to convince the client of the irrationality of his thoughts and to reveal errors in his perception of himself. The client was instructed in the manner in which his thought processes were making him unhappy and neurotic. These thoughts were attacked and contradicted and a more rational philosophy of life was internalized by the client.

Bibliotherapy   This procedure is an instructional technique using textual material, such as novels, plays, stories, booklets, etc. Through identification with the characters in a story, some clients, with counselor aid, are able to gain some understanding to resolve their problems and attain their goals. The method is as follows: (a) the counselor selects some textual material which reflects the client's needs or situation; (b) the client reads and identifies with the character in the story; (c) the client projects himself into the story; (d) the client reacts emotionally as he reads; (e) the client discusses with the counselor what he has read and how he has reacted to what he has read; and (f) the client gains insight into himself.

There are numerous ways in which this procedure may be used, depending on identified goal, age, and sex of client, and available textual material.

Thought Interference   This technique is based on the assumption that cognitive thought processes sometimes inhibit behavior. By "talking to oneself," a client can distort reality and make a predicament seem almost unbearable and unmanageable. By breaking up these thoughts and self-talk, the counselor can help the client to replace them with more realistic self-talk. This technique can lessen the inhibitory thought processes by inhibiting them. The following case is illustrative of this procedure:

Case six. Ellen, a twenty-three-year-old graduate student, came to the counseling center because she realized how unhappy she was with her social life. Her major concern was that she felt she was never going to get married. She felt she was going to end up "an old maid." Ellen had not had a date since high school that had not been "arranged" by her friends. Recently, rather than accept such arrangements, she made excuses that she was ill or had too much work to do.

It became apparent that she anticipated the worst in every situation with men. She was afraid she would "do the wrong thing," "say something dumb," "look stupid," etc. She would end up so anxious that she would do or say whatever it was she wanted so much not to do or say.

The procedure used was thought interference. The client was instructed to close her eyes and verbalize a typical problem causing thought sequence. This sequence was then abruptly interrupted by the counselor with the command, "STOP!" Through the repetition of this procedure, and the client forcing herself to concentrate on other thoughts after the stop command, she learned how to stop, by self-command, to change the direction of her thinking. This in turn, in real situations, helped to decrease her anxiety, thereby permitting her to behave in a more comfortable manner.

Assertive Training   This procedure may be used with a person who is inhibited in his expression of emotions, either positive or negative. Through inhibition, a person becomes anxious. This procedure will help a client to say the things he feels he wants to express, reducing inhibition by the practice of responses that reduce anxiety. Eventually, the anxiety response habit will be weakened and will be replaced with more adaptive behavior.

In the context of situations which represent problem areas for the client, the client practices making responses to the counselor, much the same as an actor practices a script. When the client is comfortable in making these responses (expressions of opinion, anger, needs, demands for rights, freedom, etc.), he should begin to make these responses in real situations which offer the client some probability for success. This success and/or failure can be worked out by the client and counselor in continuous interactions over the time of counseling.

Case seven. Carl, age thirty-two, could not say "no" to anyone. Three recent situations upset him very much. First, he had purchased three shirts from a salesman in a men's store, even though his shirt size was not in stock. Second, Carl was walking through a furniture store and within a few minutes had purchased a color television, which he could not afford. Lastly, the client was demoted from head coach at a junior high school because his superintendent thought that that was what he desired; Carl did not have the courage to see the superintendent and make his real wish—to remain as head coach—known to him.

Using these three situations, Carl and the counselor set up these situations in counseling and practiced making initial appropriate responses. Carl also practiced ways in which to remedy situations he had gotten into. One corrective response was decided on for each situation and was practiced until the client could behave in counseling accordingly. Carl then proceeded, with much success, in returning the shirts, canceling the television order, and straightening out the superintendent's misconceptions of what he desired.

Aversion Training   This procedure involves the use of progressive relaxation and sensitization. Rather than the goal being to reduce anxiety, as in desensitization, the goal is to increase anxiety toward a particular stimulus, thereby developing an aversion to the stimulus. The first step is the use of the procedure of Progressive Relaxation. When the client is able to relax, he is instructed to imagine a scene in which he is behaving in an undesirable manner. This scene is made as vivid as possible by the counselor's insistence on great detail. As the client begins to relate the undesirable manner in which he is about to behave in the scene, the counselor introduces some aversion to his behavior, such as the client becoming embarrassed or nauseous. This scene, and the aversion at the time of the onset of the client's undesirable behavior, is repeated several times in each counseling session and at least twice a day by the client himself.

Case eight. Charles, age twenty-three, was in counseling because of his compulsive eating habits. He weighed 248 pounds, had no social life, and was generally unhappy. Charles's goal was to learn to control his eating habits. He kept a record of everything he ate and drank between each counseling session. Particular attention was given to the kind and amount of food, and when and where he ate. Having been successfully trained in Progressive Relaxation, aversion training was applied to all types of sweets, and then to between-meal eating. The following was an example of the type of aversive instruction used:

> I want you to imagine you've just had dinner and you are about to eat your dessert, which is apple pie. As you are about to reach for the fork you get a funny feeling in the pit of your stomach. You start to feel queasy, nauseous, and sick all over. As you touch the fork, you can feel the food particles inching up your throat. You're just about to vomit. As you put the fork into the pie, the food comes up into your mouth. You're bringing the

piece of pie to your mouth. As you are about to open your mouth you vomit. [*This description of the vomiting scene will continue in vivid detail including the smell and shocked expression of others at the table.*] At this point you turn away from the food and immediately start to feel better. You run out of the room, and as you run, you feel better and better.

Charles was instructed to repeat this scene at least twice a day between sessions. Equal time was spent in aversion training to sweets and in positive reinforcement, as praise, pleasant imagery, when the client did not eat the food. The same procedure was used for Charles's between-meal-eating habits.

Principle 2—People Learn to Behave in New Ways by Imitating the Behavior, Beliefs, Values, and Attitudes of Significant Others   This principle accounts for much of the development and change of human behavior, including language development, motor skills, attitudes, values, beliefs, and emotions. The significant other, then, is described as a model who will be emulated by the learner. There are a number of factors which can influence a given person to emulate another. Clearly, the relationship to the learner is an influencing factor. The closer the relationship, the more likely is the potential model to be emulated. Another set of influencing factors has to do with the characteristics of the potential model. He is more likely to be emulated if he is seen by the learner as a person of high status and prestige. Further, a learner is likely to emulate those actions of a person known as an expert. Novice sports enthusiasts learn to play the sport by emulating the actions of those who are considered to be experts in the field.

Yet another influencing factor has to do with the *instrumental value* of certain behavior. People who are not functioning effectively learn to do so by observing others and copying their behaviors; this is seen as instrumental to the attainment of goals and important to the learner. The principle in Chapter 2, that human behavior is purposive and goal directed, is especially applicable here. A high school student, for example, who has difficulty making and maintaining friends, may observe his peers, identify with those who make and maintain friends easily, and then try to emulate their friendship behavior.

A counselor may also help his client learn to function more effectively by identifying himself as a model who can be emulated, and then behaving in those ways which he believes will be instrumental to the effective functioning of his client. This situation was demonstrated earlier where a counselor helped a client relax by identifying himself as a model and then taking on a relaxed appearance.

Two other dimensions worthy of further discussion are covert vs. overt modeling, and direct vs. vicarious modeling. In overt modeling situations, all people involved are aware that persons learn by imitating others. Such would be the case in role-play situations, used frequently in both individual and group counseling. Under covert modeling situations, the learner is not aware that his behavior is being influenced à la the imitative tendency. Such appeared to be the case in the example where the client learned unconsciously to relax by imitating the counselor.

Under direct modeling conditions, the learner emulates a model in his immediate environment. Under vicarious or indirect modeling conditions, the learner observes a second person who, himself, is imitating a third person (the model). Take, for example, the case of a child who demonstrates strong fear of water. Application of vicarious modeling, as a counseling strategy, would occur if the counselor were to make a video tape of another person who demonstrates a fear of water while he is watching his peers jumping in and out of the water, splashing around, and generally demonstrating the fun of such activity. The scene would then be played back to the client; what is observed would be discussed in counseling. This example also demonstrates a potential application of video technology in the counseling process, a strategy that is currently receiving much attention in counseling literature.

Some specific case studies will help to demonstrate the actual application of some of these principles in the counseling process. The case studies will describe:

1. The use of role playing.
2. The maintenance of the counseling relationship.
3. The use of media to present models.

The Use of Role Playing   The use of this modeling technique enables the client to gain understanding of himself and others in his environment, to determine how he may modify his behavior in a given environment, and to practice the modified behaviors that he desires. The proper use of the role-playing technique can lead to specific and accurate changes in the client's behavior.

The first step in the use of this procedure is the assignment of roles. This step, of course, is subsequent to the identification of the goal of counseling, problem definition, and appropriate selection of the method of aid in helping the client to arrive at his goal. In the setting, the counselor assigns himself the role of the significant other while the client plays himself. The counselor may portray the client's father, boss, spouse, or anyone else who is involved with the client at the time when the client desires to modify his behavior. Following this portrayal, the roles of each are analyzed in an attempt to gain some understanding of the dynamics that operate in the setting. After this analysis is completed, the next step is to reverse the roles, whereby the counselor portrays the client and the client plays the significant other person. The next step is to analyze these roles with an attempt to aid the client in understanding the position and feelings of the significant other. The final step is to determine what the client desires to do differently in the setting. These client behavioral changes would be practiced, via role playing and role reversal, until the client behaves in the counseling-role situation desired. When the client behaves with ease in this different role, he is instructed to try it out in a real environmental setting. Further counseling time may be necessary to modify the new role after it has been attempted.

This procedure may use people other than the counselor to play roles. Actual props are sometimes necessary, such as telephones for conversation. In general, the rule to be followed is to approach the real setting in terms of people, equipment, and situational props. The following successful cases are illustrative of this procedure:

Case nine. Al had had a long series of unsuccessful job experiences, most periods of employment lasting only a few months. Early in counseling, he stated that his major problem was his explosive temper, usually directed toward authority and especially his on-the-job supervisors. After spending some time with the client, the counselor concurred that this was the area that was of most concern. The procedure selected to help Al to modify his behavior was that of role playing.

Al played himself while the counselor portrayed an on-the-job supervisor in a confrontation which enabled both to gain insight into Al's behavior. Discussion followed. The second step was to reverse the roles, thereby helping the client to gain some understanding of the supervisor's reaction to Al. The client then generated other ways he could behave and settled on one which was more desirable in the situation under consideration. This was practiced repeatedly over a two-week period. The new behavior became the usual behavior for the client in a confrontation situation with his superiors.

Case ten. Joe came to counseling for help in learning to meet and talk with girls. A senior in high school, he had become aware that in social situations, he experienced a good deal of difficulty interacting with members of the opposite sex. This awareness added to the client's concern, making him even more uneasy and anxious in the problem situations than he was previously. The counselor, a man, decided to use the role-playing technique. After portraying roles, reversing roles, and helping the client to feel more at ease in situations, the office secretary was asked to become a part of the counseling procedure. She portrayed herself while Joe played himself with the help of prompts by the counselor. These prompts were counselor responses which the client was encouraged to imitate. When imitated effectively, Joe was reinforced by the counselor with verbal approval. This was repeated, various environments were staged, and the prompting decreased and finally stopped. Joe was instructed to go out of his way to speak with girls. Finding this difficult at first, with the counselor's continued support over a two-week period, Joe met with success and was finally able to handle these situations with ease.

Case eleven. Janet was completing the requirements for a teaching degree and was apprehensive about being interviewed for a job. She feared that she would say the wrong thing, feel nervous, and be unable to give a favorable impression of herself to the interviewer. Role-playing situations were contrived and acted out. Janet learned how to behave with a variety of interviewers—formal, friendly, casual, etc., and how to put herself in the most favorable light for the position for which she was applying.

The Maintenance of the Counseling Relationship   At times, the simple continuance of a good human relationship is a counseling procedure in and of itself. This relationship has been characterized by counselor behaviors of empathic understanding, warmth, genuineness, honesty, and professionalism. These characteristics, and the counselor behaviors necessary for their attainment, have been discussed in Chapter 4.

The basic concept in using the relationship as a modeling procedure is *to the extent that the client has regard and respect for the counselor, will, in all probability result in the client becoming more like the counselor.* This procedure works effectively with client problems, such as the inability to converse with others in a meaningful manner; the inability to express one's feelings; the manner of approaching personal relationships in a cool or distrustful manner; and being a "phoney." After such a behavior change goal is established, and the counselor selects this technique for helping the client reach his goal, the counselor then maintains and intensifies the relationship.

As the relationship intensifies, the counselor acts as the model for the client. By emulating counselor behavior, the client learns new ways of behaving toward others, including the *client* use of listening, attentive behaviors, and reflective response leads to affect others. The end result is that the client, while behaving in new ways, would be able to converse with others in a meaningful manner, express his feelings to others, approach personal relationships in a warm and trusting manner, and learn to be, and behave like, himself.

The Use of Media to Present Models   This technique encompasses the use of all audio or audiovisual media to present models to be imitated. The procedure is similar to that of bibliotherapy except the material used is not textual by itself, but includes the use of audiovideo presenters, such as audio tapes, phonograph records, video tapes, and films. The method is as follows: (a) the counselor selects some audio or audiovisual material in which the model used reflects the client's need or situation; (b) the client listens and watches the presentation and identifies with the model; (c) the client discusses with the counselor what he has seen; and (d) the client tries the new, learned behavior with the counselor (role playing), and finally, in the real life situation.

The basic principle that people learn by imitating others is well documented in research literature. However, counseling research has only begun to explore the parameters and the potential application of these notions to the counseling process. While it is doubtful that application of such basic principles as these will ever be considered a panacea to counseling, it is important to recognize that the counselor who identifies himself as a model likely to be emulated, whether he is aware of it or not, can systematically utilize this principle to enhance his counseling effectiveness.

Any counselor identifying himself as a model must also accept the responsibility for doing so. This responsibility includes an awareness on his part of his behaviors, attitudes, values, and beliefs that the client may emulate. He must come to grips with the issue of whether it is in the client's best interest to acquire these new behaviors, and to think through whether he has a right to influence the client, often without the client's awareness.

Principle 3—The Reinforcement Contingencies in a Person's Environment Influence the Way He Behaves in That Environment. Changing the Reinforcement Contingencies Can Be Expected to Influence a Change in Behavior   This is, of course, the operating credo of an effective conditioning system. Systematic application of this principle in the counseling situation demands thorough comprehension of all the basic concepts and laws of learning described by this system. To articulate this system in comprehensive detail would be beyond the scope of this book. Briefly, systematic application of this system demands understanding of the following concepts: reinforcement, punishment, extinction, discrimination, generalization, target behavior, shaping, successive approximation, and schedules of reinforcement.

Application of operant conditioning principles is clearly consistent with the basic assumption that human behavior is purposive and goal directed. The applier of such principles must begin with a clear description of what new behaviors he wants the client to acquire. He must then determine what environmental events will serve as effective reinforcers for his client; that is, what goals are important for his client to attain. Following this, the counselor must determine how he can control the occurrence of these reinforcers so as to shape the desired behaviors. He must also consider the additional effects of systematically applying the principles which will be described later in this chapter.

It is necessary to discuss several types of environmental consequences. Those consequences which achieve a desired "input" for the client (approval, candy, money, successful completion of an important task) may be described as "positive reinforcers." Those consequences which achieve a non-desired input (verbal chastisement, disapproval, physical pain) are described as "punishment," or negative reinforcers. Behaviors which result in positively reinforcing consequences will increase in likelihood or frequency. But behaviors which result in punitive consequences generally do not decrease in likelihood or frequency; their occurrence is only temporarily suppressed.

Sometimes the counselor can control the environment so that behaviors result in no intended external consequences. If that occurs consistently, the behavior can generally be expected to decrease in likelihood or frequency. That process is referred to as *extinction.* At other times, people will behave in ways so as to *avoid* unpleasant or disastrous consequences. If their behavior does result in the avoidance of such consequences, it can be expected to increase in frequency or likelihood when similar situations occur again. This is the process of *avoidance conditioning.*

In order to use reinforcement techniques in counseling, the counselor must be aware of (1) the operant, and (2) appropriate rewards. The *operant* is that client behavior which the counselor will reinforce. For the strongest learning effect on the client, the client must freely exhibit the operant to be reinforced. Ideally, the counselor should wait patiently for the operant. However, the counselor can use *successive approximations;* that is, begin rewarding client behavior that is close to the desired behavior. Then, in a step-by-step process, lead the client to the appropriate behavior. Another approach would be the counselor's use of interpretive response leads to get the client to behave as desired. In any event, it is important that the client exhibit the desired behavior on his own. Once he does, the counselor can reward the client for this behavior.

In the context of a counseling situation, most counselors systematically include such principles in their intervention strategy and base their approach on the application of positive reinforcement principles. They would ask themselves, "What kinds of environmental events would serve as effective positive reinforcers for this particular client?" and, "How may I then systematically control those positively reinforcing events?" For very young clients, tangible and consumable reinforcers seem very effective (candy, little toys, and trinkets). For older people, some sort of positive social input seems to have a powerful reinforcing effect (genuine attention, approval, recognition, etc.). For many people, successful completion of a challenging task seems to have a powerful reinforcing effect.

Most often two or more of these basic operant conditioning principles are applied simultaneously. The counselor views the client as currently using inappropriate or undesirable behaviors in certain situations. In those situations, certain other behaviors would be more appropriate, effective or desirable. Thus, the counselor has two related tasks: first, eliminating the inappropriate behavior from the person's behavioral repertoire using some sort of extinction-based process, and second, simultaneously establishing the new and more desirable behaviors in the person's repertoire, generally using some sort of positive reinforcement-based process (see case twelve below).

With some clients, the difficulty is not so much that they are generally behaving inappropriately, but that they are using certain behaviors that are appropriate in certain situations but inappropriate in others. Helping people learn to distinguish between those occasions or situations in which certain actions are appropriate and those in which the same actions are not is the process of *discrimination training*. Using such a strategy, the counselor's task is to help the client learn under which conditions a given action is appropriate. Usually such a strategy is based on helping the person identify the ways in which the two or more situations involved differ from each other. Once the differences between situations have been learned, the task then is to help the person learn to behave appropriately.

The following reinforcement counseling techniques will be reviewed in order to demonstrate the methods of this procedure:

1. Operant conditioning
2. Successive approximation of goal
3. Positive attention
4. Extinction through non-reinforcement
5. Discrimination training

Operant Conditioning This technique is characterized by the direct rewarding of specific client behavior. Specific behavior is directly related to the goal of counseling as established by the client with the aid of the counselor. The following case is illustrative of the use of this technique.

Case twelve. Dwayne, a college senior, was having difficulty making friends. It became obvious to the counselor that this client "turned others off" by the manner in which he spoke of himself. Continually using negative self-references and "running himself down," Dwayne could understand why others didn't like him ("I'm just not much to know"), but desired to change in order to give others an opportunity to get to like him.

The client spent some time in relating his home life while growing up, and, with the aid of the counselor, gained some understanding for his self-deprecation. Gradually, the counselor began to reinforce Dwayne's positive self-references. The counselor did this by showing attention, holding eye contact, and verbally expressing his pleasure when the client said good things about himself. These attentive vocal and nonvocal counselor behaviors were not used when Dwayne verbalized negative things about himself. Over the course of seven sessions, Dwayne made more and more positive references about himself, and found that this carried over into his daily contacts. The client was pleased with his success, related to the counselor that others were more pleased with him, and, in general, stated that he "felt a good deal better about himself and so did others."

Successive Approximation of Goal   This technique employs the use of a step-by-step method of arriving at the desired goal. After the goal has been established, and the input of the client, in terms of the goal, has been measured, a course of action using sequential steps to the goal is developed by the counselor with the aid of the client. The following case was successful and illustrates the method for successive approximation of goal.

Case thirteen. Lisa, ten years of age, had a great fear of water and would not play in the family pool. By using successive approximations, the counselor helped Lisa to enjoy the pool. Beginning with a familiarity of the pool area by playing near the pool, through successive approximations—feet in water, splashing feet, hands in water, sitting on pool steps, etc., to the goal of complete submersion—the counselor successfully helped Lisa to accomplish her goal by using the counselor as friend and play partner as the reinforcer.

Positive Attention   This simple technique is based on the reinforcement potential of positive attention, while ignoring all unwanted behaviors. The following case demonstrates the successful use of this procedure by a classroom teacher under the consultative direction of a counselor:

Case fourteen. Phil was an eleven-year-old boy who was considered an "acting-out child" in the classroom. He would wander around the room, disrupt group activities, and become angry when corrected or disciplined. Phil's test results showed he had average intelligence, but he was doing poorly in his school subjects. Phil stated to the counselor that he wished he didn't have to act the way he did, but didn't know of any other way to behave. He admitted that he enjoyed the attention his disruptive behavior brought him. The counselor, consulting with the teacher, and with his help, used Phil's need for attention to help him change his manner of behaving. The teacher gave Phil positive attention whenever he was working at his desk quietly or whenever he was behaving in a socially acceptable manner in a group activity. This helped Phil to satisfy this need for attention while successfully modifying his behavior.

Extinction Through Non-reinforcement   A behavior that at one time was rewarding can be modified by changing the reward structure so that it is no longer rewarding to behave in that manner. In other words, a behavior which is not reinforced will be extinguished and replaced by a more rewarding behavior.

Case fifteen. Bobby, age five, was brought to the counseling center because of poor speech development. He spoke very little and used only single words and phrases; mostly, he made his wants known through gestures and grunts. A physician felt that there was no organic basis for this problem. Bobby's development in other areas had been normal. The goal of therapy was to change Bobby's nonverbal behavior into verbal behavior.

Observations of the family interaction and interviews led to the assumption that Bobby's nonverbal behavior was being reinforced. Bobby had, in effect, three mothers caring for him and anticipating his every need—his mother and two sisters, ages thirteen and fifteen. He had no need to speak. A gesture brought him what he wanted.

All the family members were instructed to become "blind" to Bobby's gestures. They were to indicate that they did not know what he wanted and that he would have to tell them. When the nonverbal behavior failed to attain reinforcement, it began to extinguish, and Bobby gradually began to use speech to request what he wanted. The successful attainment of goals occurred, which in turn reinforced his speech behavior.

Discrimination Training   Behavior does not simply "occur." People respond to situations, and appropriate behavior depends in part on the particular situation. Sometimes people generalize behavior as being appropriate in one situation but not in another situation. Often behaviors are overgeneralized. The more similar two situations are, the more likely there will be generalization. As the following case demonstrates, the intended impact of discrimination training is to help the client distinguish between two situations, so that the behavior in one situation will not be used to generalize another situation in which it would be inappropriate. The basis of the strategy is to help the client identify the differences between the two situations.

Case sixteen. Eleanor, in her mid-forties, had been divorced and had remarried. Her first husband treated her cruelly, to the point where she learned to respond in his presence with considerable fear and anxiety. She also generalized this fear response to other situations. Even discussing her husband, long after the divorce, evoked strong fear. The woman had enrolled in a course attended by about fifteen students. The instructor required considerable interaction in the classroom between the students and himself. The woman responded with strong fear toward the instructor, and since the course required classroom interaction, she was clearly experiencing considerable difficulty. Upon discussion, it became clear that she was generalizing the fear responses she had learned with her husband with that of the instructor. Many of the apparent physical features of the instructor and her husband appeared similar to her. The counselor then asked the woman to describe some ways in which the two men were dissimilar. As she talked, she found more and more ways in which they were different from each other. She later met with the instructor and continued to focus on these differences. During a follow-up session, she reported that the differences between the two men were quite apparent, especially with respect to their behavior toward her, and that she no longer was responding with strong fear. The entire discrimination learning process took approximately ten to fifteen minutes.

Principle 4—Some People Learn to Function More Effectively by Becoming Aware of Certain Characteristics About Themselves or Their Environments   Awareness, as a major concept in the counseling process, was introduced in Chapter 2. A major point was that for certain clients (those who are quick to grasp abstractions, non-defensive, and able to relate abstractions to appropriate behavior) facilitating awareness may be a powerful way to help achieve certain kinds of outcome goals. While many theorists have agreed that awareness was an important process goal, they seemed to disagree about the specific kinds of phenomena they wanted their clients to become aware of.

To the writers of this book, the essential issue can be expressed by raising a series of interrelated questions: Awareness of what will lead to what kinds of changes with what kinds of clients? Giving a specific client and his characteristics a particular goal, what kinds of awareness will help him achieve his outcome goal? If a client is helped to achieve awareness of specific things, what impact will occur? While research in human behavior is a long way from attaining definitive answers to these vital questions, what assumption may be made that awareness of some sort is a valuable process goal for clients with a variety of outcome goals? It will be useful to distinguish between awareness of self-related characteristics and awareness of environmental characteristics.

It is from this point on that counseling becomes most judgmental, complex, and least amenable to structure. For any given client with any specific goal, we simply cannot be certain which (if any) kinds of awareness will be of maximum favorable impact. Thus, the approach will be to help the reader consider some of the specific kinds of awareness he may wish his client to become aware of, and some of the potential impacts. In a sense, the approach will be to generate some interesting alternatives. Which alternatives (or combination of alternatives) depend upon the goals and characteristics of the client, and the talents of the counselor.

For some clients, especially those desiring to make career and/or educational decisions, awareness of specific skills, talents, aptitudes, and interests will be essential. For some, awareness of demand characteristics of the environment will be especially impactful. For others, awareness of values and beliefs will have important instrumental value. For clients having interpersonal difficulties, awareness of how one's behavior affects significant others would appear essential (i.e., aware of the interpersonal consequences of one's actions). Similarly, awareness of the impact of the behavior of others would appear to be of real value to a client having these problems.

We may borrow from the basic notions of Chapter 2 to generate some important client awareness. In that chapter, we indicated an essential assumption: that human behavior is purposive and goal directed. From that assumption, we can make some important corollary statements. Effective functioning is directly influenced by the clarity, accuracy and specificity with which an individual identifies his goals. The more clearly, accurately, and specifically a person identifies his goals, the more effectively he is likely to function. One reason individuals fail to function as effectively as they might otherwise is that they have not identified clearly the goals they are trying to attain. Thus, becoming aware of the really important goals they are striving for may be seen as a major desirable process goal for many clients. Counselor responses, such as the following, are especially helpful in facilitating this dimension of awareness:

"If you had the best of all possible situations, what would you like to accomplish most?"

"In contrast to the way things are now, how would you most like them to be?" "Are you sure?"

"How will both of us know when counseling has been successful?" "What criteria should we use to determine such success?"

Given a client who is aware that his behavior is maladaptive, but is confused as to why it persists, a counselor might wish to respond: "If you are behaving this (undesirable) way even though you do not want to, perhaps it is because there is a purpose to your behavior. That is, your actions are probably attaining some desirable goals for you. Can you think how your actions might be paying off for you?" Clearly, the intended goal of these counselor responses is to help the client become more aware of the intended goals of his actions.

Another assumption associated with any given action indicated in Chapter 2 is a set of consequences. As a corollary, it may also be said that effective functioning depends upon an individual's ability to accurately anticipate the consequences (immediate and delayed; observable and nonobservable) of his actions. The more consequences he can accurately anticipate, and the more accurately he can anticipate consequences, the more effectively he is likely to function. Thus, helping a client become aware of the actual consequences of his previous actions and the potential consequences of his future actions represents additional potential awareness-based process goals. To achieve this impact, the counselor may wish to consider some form of the following responses:

"Given the situation you described, and the particular people who were involved, what do you think happened as a consequence of your actions?" Assuming a reasonably accurate description of consequences, the counselor might then say: "Were you glad about those consequences?" Assuming the client failed to indicate some important consequences, the counselor might follow up by saying: "What other consequences might also have occurred?"

"What things might happen as a consequence if you were to do the things you say you might do?" "Would you feel glad or upset about those consequences?"

"Given that you did not like what happened in the situation you are describing, what consequences would you have preferred?"

The intended impacts of these counselor responses are two: To help the client become more fully aware of important consequences, and to become more fully aware of how he *values* those consequences. As indicated in Chapter 2, the *valuing* of consequences is a process equally as important as the *anticipation* of the consequences.

The interrelationship among three important constructs should be clearly identified: desired goals, actions, and consequences. People are said to be functioning effectively when the actual consequences of their actions are in agreement with their desired goals. However, people frequently behave in such ways that the actual consequences of their actions are incongruent and incompatible with their desired goals. The adolescent male who wants acceptance and regard from his peers, but who relates to them with constant bullying tactics, is a good example. It is likely that his peers will reject him as a consequence of such bullying actions. Another example is of the student who is caught cheating. His goal was to do well on the exam; he attained his goal. But the additional consequences which occurred were strongly negative.

Helping people become aware of the interrelationships between desired goals, actions, and actual consequences is a major set of process goals. An essential part of this process is to help the client search for, become aware of, and implement new alternatives which will more effectively achieve desired goals and/or result in less negative consequences. Counselor responses, such as those indicated above, help facilitate this awareness-based process. Here are some additional potential responses:

"Given that we have looked at the consequences of your actions, do you think you really achieved your desired goals?"

"From what you say, it would seem that what actually occurred was opposite to what you really wanted. Can you think of some different ways you could have handled the situation so that you might have attained what you really wanted?"

"Given what you want, and the way you say you intend to get what you want, what additional consequences might occur if you were to go ahead with your plan? How would you feel if those additional consequences were to occur? Can you think of some other possible plans where you could get what you want without the negative consequences?"

Another level of awareness refers to awareness of emotions. This process may be described by borrowing from the basic *S-R* (stimulus-response) paradigm as well as from the notions on emotions in Chapter 2. Looking at emotions first, it may be said that for any given individual, specific emotional responses are more likely to occur in certain kinds of situations. Further, the intensity of any given emotion may depend on a specific situation. Thus, helping a client become aware of the dominant emotions he tends to experience, the intensity of given kinds of emotions he tends to experience, and the situation in which these are likely to occur may be an especially impactful awareness-based process goal. Take, for example, the following client response (adolescent male, high school, second interview): "It's because I'm black. People don't come right out and say it, but I know deep down they look down on me and treat me as if I were inferior. I really resent that." A valuable process goal might be to help the client become aware of the strong resentment, anger, bitterness, and hostility he feels, and the situations in which he feels that way. Later on, another counseling process goal may be to help him learn to cope with his feelings and the situations identified. An impactful counselor response might be: "I guess those feelings of anger and resentment are things you feel often and very strongly. Can you tell me about some specific times you felt especially bitter and resentful?"

We may also begin with the other element in the paradigm to provide a slightly different approach to the facilitation of emotion awareness. Certain situations elicit given emotions. Further, the intensity of those emotions depend in a large part on the situation. Thus, helping a client become aware of certain important situations and the kinds and intensity of emotions elicited by those situations is another potential awareness-based process goal. An example might be of an adolescent girl who discusses her relations with authority figures and communicates her difficulty in these relationships, but gives no more specific information than that. The counselor who responds with, "It seems that whenever you are with people who have power and control over you, some very strong feelings occur and you have difficulty controlling them. Could you tell me specifically the kinds of feelings you have in these situations?" is trying to help the client gain this kind of awareness. Once the feelings are identified, the counselor can help the client become aware of the way those feelings affect her ability to cope with and relate to such people. The client's awareness will offer important clues as to desirable outcome goals and important notions to the counselor as how to be of valuable help to his client.

Clearly, the two emotion-awareness approaches are not incompatible, and both are frequently considered desirable for many clients who are capable of awareness. Note that in both cases the counselor's response followed the same basic format. He first identified or reflected what he heard, and then responded with a CTRL (Counselor Tacting Response Lead) whose purpose was to help the client (and himself) become aware of the relationship between situations and intense feelings. For many clients, the process is one of dominant emotions to the situations in which they are likely to occur, and important situations to the dominant emotions they are likely to elicit. Once such relationships are identified, a major process goal might be to change those undesirable relationships.

An area of counseling where awareness becomes especially essential is in the decision-making process. The following describes the decision-making process and relates awareness facilitation to that process.

Principle 5—Some People Learn to Function More Effectively by Acquiring a Specific Method for Decision Making   A major domain of counselors is to help clients make important decisions which will have impact on what happens to them in the future. Choices regarding current and future educational plans, occupation, and marriage and the family are major decision areas for which people regularly seek the help of counselors.

Some decisions are made on impulse, with no thought or consideration of the consequences. A woman who sees a dress in a store window and exclaims, "I must have that dress! The price doesn't matter. Whether my husband will like it doesn't matter!" might be a good example. Another person might order a meal in a restaurant ("I feel like having steak tonight"). Other decisions are automatic—almost a reflex action. Little thought is involved in stopping at a red traffic light. Other decisions, especially those made by people who seek the help of counselors, require much more thought and discussion. There is a methodology or process by which such decisions are arrived at, and implied in that methodology are some important process goals for helping clients make important decisions.

The methodology of the decision-making process is that of: identifying the problem; determining goals; describing existing conditions related to the problem; generating all potential alternatives; predicting the likelihood of all possible consequences (immediate and delayed; observable and nonobservable); value judging the desirability of all possible consequences of each alternative; selecting; implementing the selected alternative and evaluating actual consequences. According to basic decision methodology, the alternative selected should be the one which will have the greatest likelihood of achieving desired goals, which will result in the least negative consequences, and which will be consistent (and not inconsistent) with basic values.

Each element in this methodology becomes a basic and necessary process goal for the fullest involvement in helping a client whose goal is to make a decision. Said another way, each element becomes a specific task which the counselor must undertake for counseling to be of maximum utility for the client. Thus, the counselor must be sure that:

1. He and the client have accurately identified the problem.
2. He has helped the client become aware of the basic goals related to the decision which the client wants to accomplish.

3. He has helped the client describe, account for, and become aware of those existing conditions which are related to the decision.
4. He has helped the client generate and become aware of all potential alternatives which will attain the identified goals.
5. He has helped the client predict and become aware of the potential consequences which might occur for each alternative if it were implemented, and the likelihood of those consequences.
6. He has helped the client become aware of his basic values related to evaluating the desirability or undesirability of the consequences he predicts.
7. He has helped the client develop a set of criteria for evaluating each alternative. The criteria developed should be a synthesis or an abstraction of: the goals identified, the conditions described, the consequences predicted, and the values identified.

Further, the counselor must help the client evaluate each alternative in light of the criteria developed above. Once this process is accomplished, the client and counselor will have hopefully narrowed the potential range of available alternatives. However, counseling is not completed. The counselor must help the client identify the steps he must take and the tasks he must accomplish to implement the alternative or alternatives selected.

It is important to analyze further some of these basic tasks. We begin with the interrelated tasks of identifying the problem and establishing the goals. Whereas a statement of a problem is usually an indication of some dissatisfying state of affairs at present, statements of goals are indications of conditions which will exist in the future, if the current problem is resolved. The high school senior may enter with a problem, such as "I can't decide which colleges to apply to, and I need some help deciding." His *problem* is, he cannot decide. His *goal* is to attend the college which is "best" for him. In a sense, counseling may be seen as the process of deciding really what is meant by "best," and a major part of the task is that of developing criteria to determine the "best" college. To accomplish this goal, client and counselor together will have to develop criteria to evaluate alternatives, identify potential alternatives, and eliminate those options which fail to satisfy the criteria developed.

Goal identification, however, goes much deeper. Attending college is only a process goal for attaining other goals, and, therefore, it is important that the client acquire some awareness of the goals beyond the goal of attending college. Such goals might include: entering into a career field for which a college education is necessary; a desire to learn and study; conformity to social norms; attainment of prestige and stature; capitulating to parental pressure; satisfying an achievement motivation; a chance to meet new people. Thus, helping a client become aware of desired goals is not a simple or superficial task. For some clients, awareness of goals may become a difficult experience.

Since "creativity" may be operationally defined as the tendency to generate new alternatives to solve a problem, it is clear that creativity is an integral part of the decision-making process. In helping an individual select from several alternatives, a major counseling task is to help the client generate potential alternatives —that is, to become creative. Choosing a college or a career is frequently referred to as the process of *exploration.* Exploration in decision-making is the process of generating alternatives, projecting oneself into each alternative, and asking oneself what consequences would occur if the given alternative were, in fact, selected. From here, the process is one of evaluating the consequences and value judging their desirability. A major part of counseling for decision-making is that of helping clients in this exploration process.

"Brainstorming" may also be understood as a facet of "generating alternatives" process. In brainstorming sessions, no alternative is evaluated until all have first been generated. The rationale is that when alternatives are evaluated too quickly certain unappealing alternatives might be too quickly rejected. The implications for decision counseling are clear.

Later in this discussion, we will relate the "alternative generating" step in the counseling process of information systems, as well as its implications for effective counseling.

"Describing existing conditions" refers to two interrelated assessment or evaluation processes: assessment of self and assessment of environment. The process of helping a client assess himself is one of helping him become aware of, and to take into account, those factors and characteristics about himself which are related to the decision problem. The process is one of facilitating *self-exploration,* the goal of which is clearly to help the client achieve greater self-awareness. The dimensions of assessment discussed in Chapter 5 may also be seen as dimensions of client awareness. Thus, self-awareness might include such things as: awareness of one's level of general intellectual development; awareness of one's level of development regarding specific skills, aptitudes, and talents; awareness of various activities (interests) one prefers to engage in; and awareness of one's dominant interpersonal characteristics.

People acquire self-awareness by comparing self with self (idiographic), and by comparing self with others (nomothetic). The counselor who helps a client ask himself, "At which activity am I more skillful—researching and reviewing published literature or writing creatively?" is helping the client make an idiographic comparison of his talents. A client asking himself, "Which do I prefer more—playing an outdoor sport or sitting at home reading?" is comparatively assessing his interests. These are the kinds of comparisons the items on the *Strong Vocational Interest Blank* and the *Kuder Preference Record* ask test takers to make. The rationale is that by engaging in such self-comparisons, an individual will become more aware of activities he prefers most and least, and then this awareness will become a major influencing factor in the process of choosing.

The counselor may facilitate such self-awareness as a natural part of his discussion with his client or he may administer tests as those described above to help initiate the self-comparison–self-awareness process. The purpose in using such tests is to help the client identify what he has discovered about himself as soon as possible after he has taken the test, and then enable him to explore how those discoveries affect his beliefs about himself. The following simulated dialogue may help to clarify this process.

Counselor 1:   Well, Ted, you came in for help in choosing a career, and we decided to help you make a sensible choice by getting you to learn more about the kinds of activities you prefer most and the kinds you prefer least. So we decided that the *Kuder Preference Record* would help you toward this goal. You took it, and then scored it yourself. Can you tell me some of the things you might have learned about your-self as you were responding to the items?

Client 1:   Gee, I'm not really sure where to begin. Could you help me get started?

Counselor 2:   Well, perhaps there were certain items that you remember especially well. Perhaps some that you couldn't an-swer easily and had to stop and think about.

Client 2:   Well. . . . Yeah, come to think about it, I guess there were a couple. Like one where the three choices were to work in an automobile plant, be in a circus, or work in crop fields. I had a lot of trouble with that one because I liked all three. I like being outdoors, I like performing in front of people, and I also like building things and putting things together. Wow, I had trouble with that one.

Counselor 3:   Um . . . hm. The problem with that item was that all the alternatives seemed appealing. Can you remember which you rated as preferring most and which you rated as preferring least?

Client 3:   Um . . . I think I put down working in a circus as most, and in an automobile shop as least.

Counselor 4:   Um . . . hm. Can you tell me the thinking
                  you went through to come to that de-
                  cision?

Client 4:   [*Pause*] Well, I figured in a circus you
               would meet a lot of people. You would
               do a lot of traveling, and see new
               places and all.

Counselor 5:   I guess that would mean that traveling
                  and meeting new people are two ac-
                  tivities you value very highly.

Client 5:   Yeah . . . that's for sure.

Counselor 6:   Well, how might that be related to your
                  thinking about a career?

Client 6:   Well, I sure would want a career where
               I would be meeting lots of new peo-
               ple. But . . . actually as I think about
               it, I probably would get tired traveling
               after awhile. I don't think I would want
               to keep traveling forever.

Several things should be clear from this dialogue. First, once the counselor had finished his introductory remarks, his responses were very short—two or three sentences. But at each choice point situation, his goal was to facilitate greater self-awareness. Each response he made was clearly to facilitate that process. He did not offer advice; he did not interpret. All his responses were to help the client introspect about himself. Second, the client came for help in career choice, so a major part of the counselor's responsibility was to relate the introspection process to the decision at hand. This he clearly did at Counselor 6. From here, the counselor helped the client go through the same process with other items on the inventory and eventually with the scales the inventory yielded.

When a client asks himself, "How do my skills as an automobile mechanic compare to those of significant others?" or "Do others prefer clerical work as much as I do?" he is involved in making nomothetic comparisons. His answers to these questions are clearly related to choices regarding future career and education. A person who wants to be an insurance salesman, for example, will want to predict as accurately as possible whether he has the necessary skills and talents to compete successfully with others in the field. Thus, he will want to know what skills and talents are related to effective performance in the field, the level of such skills related to success, whether it is a highly competitive business, and the level of the skills held by those identified as being successful.

Thus, part of the process goal identified as "describing existing conditions" is really the process of self-assessment, self-exploration, and self-awareness. An essential part of the task is gathering information about self. The two basic information sources are recollection of behavior in past experiences, and scores on various kinds of test instruments.

"Describing existing conditions" also refers to the process of identifying and becoming aware of those environmental factors that are important to take into account in reaching a decision. This is really a two-step process: first, identifying important environmental characteristics for consideration; and second, identifying the desirable "level" of each characteristic. To the high school senior who wants to attend college, the size of the student body may be an important characteristic of colleges to consider. However, even if the student has done this, he has only accomplished the first step: identifying an important characteristic. The second step is equally important: determining what college size is desirable.

In essence, the client is developing a set of criteria to use in exploring and evaluating potential alternatives. He will consider those alternatives which satisfy his criteria and reject those which do not. If he generates no alternatives which meet his criteria, then he must reevaluate the criteria to determine which he is willing to sacrifice. This phase of decision making is basically an elimination process. Those alternatives which do not meet given criteria are eliminated. Since each new criterion eliminates options, clients may easily develop criteria for which no alternatives qualify. When this happens, the client must decide which criteria are least important. As he disposes of a given criterion, more alternatives become viable. The process of evaluating and reevaluating criteria is part of the process of value clarification. Basically, the client is asking, "Of all the criteria I have specified, which is least important for me to consider?" and "Which do I feel I can most easily give up and still be satisfied with my choice?"

Basically, this is the process which computer-assisted information systems take the client through. They suggest characteristics and ask the client if the given characteristic is important (and if so, what "level"). As the client indicates each characteristic, the computer scans its total repertoire of alternatives and indicates how many options still qualify. With each characteristic, more options are eliminated. When a certain maximum remains, the client may inquire about the remaining alternatives. The information system then indicates those alternatives which satisfy all criteria, and gives basic information about each alternative.

Below are listed some of the most important college-related characteristics students may wish to consider in choosing a college:

Region
Major fields of study
Type of school
Cost
Student body characteristics (size, average entrance scores, etc.)
Accreditation
Enrollment size
Source of control
Prerequisites
Application deadline
Financial aid possibilities
Special programs and services available
Campus life
Athletic programs
Prestige value

The process of helping a client develop criteria to evaluate alternative careers is basically the same. The dimensions to take into account will, of course, differ. Below are some of the career-related characteristics a counselor may wish to help his client consider:

1. Financial rewards.
2. Nonfinancial rewards (e.g., the reward of helping others, as in medicine, counseling, teaching).

3. Opportunity for advancement and promotion.
4. Skills and talents necessary to do well in various given career fields.
5. Demand characteristics (what is expected of an individual working in a given career field).
6. Future stability of the various fields considered.
7. Job security.
8. Job stress.
9. Kinds of relationships which significant others demand.
10. Effect of career choice on outside job situations (e.g., effect on one's family of working in a given field).
11. Values demanded for good performance and its relationship to one's own core values (e.g., if one values honesty, can he do a good job and not feel guilty as a key member in, say, an advertising agency).

While further analysis of this process is beyond the scope of this work, it is worth noting that simulation procedures are being used more and more to help clients project themselves into various career fields and evaluate the potential in that field. The specific kinds of stress inherent in a given career field are decision-relevant factors frequently overlooked by both clients and counselors. Medicine, teaching, selling on a commission basis, truck driving, construction work, and engineering each has its unique source of stress. Yet people in the process of choosing are rarely aware of the specific kinds of stress associated with these career fields. Rarely, too, are they helped to become aware of how they would respond to such stresses. Full counseling with clients in the process of choosing includes helping them become aware of such stresses and how they would respond to them. Video and film simulations would appear to have potential in helping clients acquire such awareness. For example, a female client interested in working as a hairdresser might be exposed to a video vignette in which a customer irately indicates to a beautician on the screen that she did a terrible job. It is clear, however, that the beautician worked hard and tried to do a conscientious job. Following this vignette, the counselor might ask the client some of the following questions:

"Suppose you were the beautician in that scene. How would you *feel* about what that customer said?"

"How would you *want* to react to her?"

"How do you think you might in fact react to her?"

"Do you think this kind of thing might happen to you as a beautician?" "How often?"

"How might your answers to yourself on these questions influence your choice about being a beautician?"

We have indicated that predicting the consequences of implementing each alternative generated earlier is a major step in decision making and in the process of decision counseling. We have indicated that this is a major part of the process of exploring alternatives. This step is related to one of the basic assumptions in Chapter 2: associated with any given action are a series of consequences.

Granted that certain consequences are delayed and others are nonobservable, this step is perhaps one of the most difficult in the decision-making process. We cannot possibly predict all the consequences of every given action. Further, prediction at the time of decision is always a matter of estimating the *likelihood* of a given consequence occurring. For any given consequence of any given alternative, we cannot accurately predict the likelihood of that consequence occurring. Thus two factors which constrain human effectiveness are: our inability to anticipate accurately all the consequences which may occur as a result of a given action; and our inability to anticipate accurately the likelihood of a given consequence. (It is from this rationale that Dewey once defined "intelligence" as the ability to anticipate accurately the consequences of one's actions.)

However, these notions suggest some ideas for effective counseling. They suggest that part of decision counseling is the process of helping a client consider potential consequences which he may not have considered. Another part is that of helping the client to more accurately estimate the *likelihood* of various consequences given an alternative for consideration. The counselor, then, should be an individual capable of helping his client more accurately predict all relevant consequences and their likelihood. To help a client become more fully aware of consequences and their likelihood means that the counselor himself must be aware of such consequences.

In decision counseling, this very difficult process may begin with a few simple counselor responses, such as: "Up to now we have looked at some alternatives, and have taken into account some criteria to evaluate these alternatives. From this we have narrowed the field down to three alternatives. Let's try to think through what might happen to you if you were to select each alternative."

Selection is a process of choosing the alternative associated with the least negative consequences. Negative consequences can be reduced, but not eliminated. If a client decides that the prestige of a college is of high value, then a consequence of choosing such a college will very likely be that he (or his family) will be forced to pay a considerable sum for tuition. If money is tight, he may have to choose a less expensive college. As a consequence, he will probably attend a less prestigious school. Thus, part of decision making is a matter of being aware of both positive and negative consequences and being prepared to cope with the negative consequences when they occur. Counseling, therefore, includes helping a client to anticipate and to cope with some potential negative consequences concerning his choice.

In this total process, the counselor will have helped the client become *aware of:* the important goals related to the decision; the factors about self and environment of the existing conditions; the alternatives available; the potential consequences and their likelihood; and important personal values related to the decision. From this, he will have helped the client become aware of criteria so that he can evaluate the alternatives identified. If the counselor is skillful and diligent, he will have helped the client to become aware of each of the steps necessary to arrive at a decision so that the client may, in the future, learn the process and implement it himself at the next important decision situation.

From the basic methodology of the decision-making process, we may develop the following checklist of process goals which will help clients with decisions:

1. Have I helped the client identify the problem?
2. Have I helped the client become aware of goals related to the decision?
3. Have I helped the client generate potential alternatives available?
4. Are there information systems available which would pro-

vide information about available alternatives? If so, have I helped the client learn to use such systems to his benefit?

5. Have I helped the client develop criteria to evaluate alternatives?

6. Have I helped the client to identify those characteristics about himself that are related to the decision?

7. If test information is available, have I helped the client to understand accurately what conclusion he can validly draw about himself and what predictions he may make from this information?

8. Have I helped the client predict and become aware of the potential consequences which might occur for each alternative, if it were implemented?

9. Have I helped the client become aware of basic values related to evaluating the desirability or undesirability of the predicted consequences?

In this process, information and information systems may be seen as helping the client perform four vital functions: identifying available alternatives; generating criteria to evaluate; anticipating potential consequences of implementing each alternative; and assessing the likelihood that each alternative can be effectively implemented. As indicated earlier, many people needing help in making decisions are not aware of the potential alternatives open to them. High school seniors who want to attend a college generally have a very limited idea of the more than 2,500 colleges which exist. People who want new careers are often not aware of potential and appealing careers available to them. To select from alternatives, one must be aware of the alternatives available. A major role of information systems is to provide data about existing alternatives. A variety of information systems is available to high school seniors wanting to choose a college. Each system is a storehouse of information, constructed in such a way that once a student has developed his criteria for choosing the system can quickly indicate to him the alternatives which satisfy these criteria. As the counselor and student develop criteria, the student becomes more aware of certain self-related characteristics. With the utilization of the information system, he is bound to come across new alternatives of which he was not previously aware.

In the college choice problem, many students may not think of enrollment size as a characteristic to take into account in developing criteria. Not only do information systems suggest this characteristic, but once an alternative is selected, the system indicates that as a consequence. For example, supposing Humangrowth U. has an enrollment of 5,000 undergraduate students, and Gaudydorm U. has an enrollment of 10,500 students, the information system will indicate to the high school senior that he will be one of 10,500 at Gaudydorm, whereas, if he chooses Humangrowth, he will be one of 5,000 students. Similarly, by indicating entrance scores on various standardized tests, information systems indicate that a given score will fall into a given range at a given college. Supposing a student's score on the SAT verbal is 550, and the mean score at Humangrowth is 650, while at Gaudydorm the mean is 500, then this information will let the student know that even if he is accepted at both places, a consequence of selecting Humangrowth would be that his score on the SAT would be well below average at that school. In contrast, a consequence of choosing Gaudydorm would be that his score would be slightly above average. Thus, the information will help him predict a consequence. The counselor's role, of course, is to help him understand the potential implications of those consequences. In this case, the counselor would want to help the client understand any possible relationship between SAT scores and college grade-point averages. He would also want to help the client ask himself whether he would function more effectively as an above-average member of a group of college students or as a below-average member.

Similarly, information helps people more accurately assess the *likelihood* of given consequences occurring as a result of an implemented choice. Expectancy tables are generally used to aid in such predictions. Suppose a test of Appliance Repairing Aptitude is developed and validated. After giving the test to all people entering this field, it was found that 95% of those scoring 50 or above remained in the field after one year, whereas only 40% of those scoring 49 or below remained after that period of time. This information would clearly help a potential entrant to predict the likelihood of his remaining in the field after one year if he chose this career field.

The purpose of this section is to help the counselor relate these ideas on the value of information systems in effective counseling. The counselor's role is not that of a walking compendium of decision-relevant information for every client. Rather, part of his role should be that of a resource person, one who knows where and how to get information easily, and how to help clients use the information in the process of making "wise" decisions. The vital part of the counselor's role is to help his client become aware of the valid conclusions, inferences, and predictions he can draw about himself from such information, and relate the new awareness to the decision at hand. In this process, the counselor must keep in mind that facilitating such self-awareness is a process goal to attain the outcome goal of making a wise decision.

Principle 6—Some People Learn to Function More Effectively by Acquiring a More Favorable Sense of Self-Esteem   A factor held by many theorists to be essential to human functioning is the concept a person has of himself. Thus, the image a person has of himself, the beliefs he maintains about himself, and his sense of self-esteem, are seen as factors which influence strongly the effectiveness with which he functions. The more favorable a person's self-image, the more effectively he is likely to function; the more negative a person's self-image, the more poorly he is likely to function. Thus, change of self-concept from negative to positive is seen as a relevant process goal for many clients, which if attained, will help many clients function more effectively.

There are several basic strategies available for changing self-concept, each based on a different set of theoretical propositions regarding that construct. The approach here will be to examine briefly the theoretical propositions and the implications these hold for potential counseling strategies.

The Phenomenological Approach   The related concepts of self-esteem and self-worth are central concepts of the phenomenological approach. This position holds that a person's sense of self-worth is based on how he is held by significant others around him. The beliefs that significant others (parents, peers, counselors) hold about an individual will influence the beliefs that that person will acquire for himself.

Thus, a person whose peers continually doubt his worth, who regard him as less than competent, who see him as an inferior, will develop a pervasive sense of self-doubt, of personal inadequacy, inferiority, and unacceptability. In contrast, a person in contact with significant others who regard him as a person of worth, worthy of respect, and capable of effective living, will acquire a favorable sense of self-esteem. Thus, the strategy of the phenomenological approach is to hold certain basic premises about an individual so that he will behave consistently with those premises. The basic assumptions about a client are, therefore, that he is a person of worth, a person whose worth is unconditional, who is entitled to be looked upon with favor, and who has an innate capacity toward favorable self-growth. To behave in a manner consistent with these principles means providing high levels of the basic core conditions (accurate empathy, nonpossessive warmth, and genuineness). Being in the presence of a person consistently supplying high levels of these core conditions will inevitably lead to the development of a more favorable self-image. Thus, the basic strategy of counselors holding these views is to continue to provide high levels of the core conditions; that is, to continue to behave consistently with the basic assumptions. What makes a counselor significantly different are the assumptions he holds and with which he behaves consistently.

Self-Concept and the Scientific Method   A very different approach to the modification of self-concept is to define self-concept as a set of theoretical statements a person makes about himself. A person's self-concept is a *theory* he holds about himself, and the principles which apply to the modification of any theoretical statement apply to the modification of theoretical statements one makes about himself. New theoretical statements are based on *data* (observable facts), and must be congruent with the facts. When data and theoretical statements are not congruent, one must be changed. The only changes possible are the search for new data which will support the existing theoretical statement or modifying the theoretical statement.

The strategy of a counselor holding this position is to help the client assess and evaluate the evidence supporting his theoretical statements, show that the evidence does not support the existing theory, and then help the client develop new theoretical statements about himself which are consistent with the evidence. Such a counselor is likely to respond at this stage of the counseling process by saying, "You know, you keep describing yourself as worthless and useless. Can you tell me the basis on which you are drawing that conclusion about yourself?" Once the client has presented the data to support this theoretical statement, the counselor is likely to respond:

> I wonder, given what you have said, is it possible to draw other conclusions about yourself? Given what you have said, I agree, we could describe you as a person who frequently makes mistakes. But from what you have said, it does not seem legitimate to describe you as useless and incompetent.

A related strategy sometimes used by the counselor is to put the client in the role of trying to prove that the counselor should accept, as truth, the theoretical statements the client is making about himself, as:

> You know, you keep talking about yourself as a useless person. That's what you believe about yourself. But that's not what I believe about you. Could you convince me that your way of seeing yourself is the way I should see you?

On the notion that a person is likely to believe what significant others tell him to say about himself, this approach is sometimes modified in the following way:

> Yes, from what you have said, it does seem that your mother thinks you are useless. But what I want to know is what *you* think of *yourself.*

The number of times clients will respond to this by saying, "Gee, I don't know. I've never really thought about it," will astound new counselors. The intended impact and ensuing strategy should be apparent from here.

Another strategy drawn from the scientific method approach is to provide new data. On the notion that continual success experi-

ences will help a person develop a favorable self-theory, counselors will sometimes structure the client's world so that he will
achieve some successful experiences. Once the client has had a
number of successful experiences, the counselor will work with
the client to help him begin to develop a more favorable theory of
self.

CASE OF BARBARA   This client identified *her* goal for counseling
in the third session: she blushes easily. The situations in which she
blushes seemed to be those that hold embarrassment or surprise
for her. Barbara is married, twenty-five years of age, and an elementary school teacher. She is about five feet in height, of slender
build, and fair-complexioned. This is the beginning of the fourth
session. After reading this, think about which potential strategies
might be implemented, the potential for success of each, and the
potential impact each might have.

Counselor: I think on Tuesday we talked a little about
your getting into certain situations and
being embarrassed and becoming very
uncomfortable. I wonder if you'd like to
continue along this line, or if there is
something else you'd rather talk about.

*Comments: Opening could have been
less structured; i.e., allowing the client
to start where she desires.*

Client: No . . . I was thinking . . . if this were a thing
of biting nails or blinking your eyes or
something like this. Well, all right, I can
—it would be hard—I could conscien-
tiously control that, but how do you control blushing?

Counselor: That's a different situation—a different reaction.

Client: It's got to be. Yeah, sort of like breaking out
in a sweat or something. I'd rather do
that. Oh, I was a very good girl yesterday
in class, I answered twice in class. . . .

Counselor: Great!

> *Comments: Reinforcement.*

Client: Yes, aren't I wonderful. . . .

Counselor: Yes, good.

Client: It's so ridiculous because I thought about it. Now, if I could just not think about it I'd be all right; something else I've thought about. I think the reason I blush is because I get self-conscious and I am very self-conscious but I think that that probably goes back to the fact of "Oh, she's so tiny. Oh, look at her, she's the tiniest little thing. Don't tell me she's really in school." And I thought of another situation and I hated this—just absolutely hated it—in another situation, a boy came into school, entered school, and I can remember this distinctly, he said, "Is she a midget?" Oh, I hated that boy, and then I had to help him with his reading. I really wasn't that small because there were other kids who were small in the class, because we always had processions and Pat and I always marched together; we were the same size. I don't think I was like three feet tall and the other kids were four. It wasn't that. I think nobody cares; I mean nobody's going to be sitting there and looking at you or picking you apart, really look you over. I know this, but I can't disengage the little feeling deep down. All right, this is what I want to know. How do you do this?

Counselor: I think maybe we're working toward that direction. I wonder if you can give me an incident where you're self-conscious?

> *Comments: CTRL for specific situation.*

Client: I thought of a couple. One I remember was during the school year, a senior girl came back. She was a senior last year and she was in my homeroom and I had her in English. She came back to see me, because she had asked me if I thought she should go to junior college in town or go away to school and, uh, I was a poor counselor—I told her what I thought 'cause she asked me. And, uh, I told her that I thought in a lot of cases it was better to go away to school. It just depended on the situation at home, but, uh, if you stayed home you didn't learn a lot of things you did when you went away to school and so she asked me to help her with her autobiography and application papers. Well, anyway, she came back—this was probably the Thanksgiving vacation—just delighted, wanted to tell me all about school, and how well she was doing. And she came into the teacher's cafeteria, and, you know, she just burst in and I never expected to see her. And the thing that kind of embarrassed me was I couldn't remember her name. That is what embarrassed me. I turned red. Then it came to me. But, well, after 130 some kids, and I had liked her very, very much and, you know, not to be able to remember her name. I knew her last name, but I couldn't think of her first name.

Counselor: But when you saw her face, your mind just went blank?

             Comments: A CRRL whose purpose is to seek clarification.

Client: No, it didn't go blank. I thought, she sat

right there in English 7, fourth period—
what is her name? No, I didn't go blank
because I remembered it by the time she
got done saying, "How are you?" and all
that. You see, when I get embarrassed,
I just light up like a neon sign. I know
other people are embarrassed. I don't
have a monopoly on it, but they don't tell
it so obviously and this I don't care for,
you see. When I think about it, I can see
again she was sort of making attention
come to me. Most people would love
that, but I don't like it. You know, everybody looked up and Diane was coming
over to sit with me and was real bubbly
and everything. I was as pleased as I
could be—but always that reaction.

Counselor: Can you tell me how you felt when she
came in—besides your being embar-
rassed.

Comments: CTRL.

Client: I just flushed. Now when I do flush most of
the time I know it. You can feel it; and
sometimes I do, but I don't even know it.
And they say, "Your face is red." And I
don't even know it. When I should know
something or I've made a mistake, I
flush. Like for instance, now I'm sitting
in a class one day, the instructor brought
in a tape recorder about a counseling
session with clients, uh, students—grade
school students. Well, it was a little bit
unorganized, anyway. And you couldn't
hear the thing. It was just the most awful
muffled thing. You really couldn't hear.
He was saying, "Wasn't this great?" and
everybody was saying, "What are they

saying?" It was just a big muddle. The acoustics were terrible. A fifth grade kid could understand but not the little kids, the tonal quality of their voices was just absolutely muffled. Now, I was thinking, that if I did something like this in class, you know, that if my record didn't work, this would embarrass me because it should have worked. I should have seen to it beforehand. This is just something I could think of where I thought I would be lit up by this time. So that would be another situation.

Counselor: You see the situation; you're being embarrassed because you felt you should have been able to. . . .

Comments: CRRL.

Client: Yeah, because I didn't. . . .

Counselor: . . . it should have run; it was supposed to.

Client: Yeah, and because I didn't say, "What the heck?" you know. I would get embarrassed. Now, if no one else were around or let's say I was at home, I might say, "Well, that stupid record player"; and I wouldn't say that in public. I'm supposed to know what I'm doing. This is just the way I feel with myself. This would be the case when it bothers me in the classroom when I really make a mistake, you see. Now I can see this, but just to meet a friend and really be glad to see them and everything, there again it's the self-consciousness, and I know this, I keep thinking when I try to control this, but then again I can't tell if I really am. I can tell if I can feel it, but I don't know.

Counselor: Now, this is flushing.

Comments: CTRL to operationally define a term.

Client: Yeah, flushing. I think, well, you know, uh, don't be self-conscious. Think about being glad to see this person and talk about them and what you want to do. Don't think about yourself. But it is hard. I am very self-conscious.

SUGGESTIONS FOR
FURTHER READING

Allen, F. H.
1942 *Psychotherapy with Children*. New York: W. W. Norton.

Axline, Virginia.
1947 *Play Therapy*. Boston: Houghton Mifflin.

1964 *Dibs: In Search of Self*. Boston: Houghton Mifflin.

Bandura, A.
1961 "Psychotherapy as a Learning Process." *Psychological Bulletin*, 58:143–159.

1969 *Principles of Behavior Modification*. New York: Holt, Rinehart and Winston.

Bandura, A. and Walters, R.
1963 *Social Imitation and Personality Development*. New York: Holt, Rinehart and Winston.

Clarke, R., Gelatt, H. B. and Levine, L.
1965 "A Decision-Making Paradigm for Local Guidance Research." *Personnel and Guidance Journal*, 44:40–51.

Dilley, J. S.
1965 "Decision-Making Ability and Vocational Maturity." *Personnel and Guidance Journal*, 44:423–427.

1967 "Decision-Making: A Dilemma and a Purpose for Counseling." *Personnel and Guidance Journal*, 45:547–551.

Ellis, A.
1962 *Reason and Emotion in Psychotherapy*. New York: Lyle Stuart.

1967 "Goals of Psychotherapy." In A. H. Mahrer, ed. *The Goals of Psychotherapy*. New York: Appleton-Century-Crofts.

Eysenck, H. J.
1960 *Behavior Therapy and the Neuroses*. London: Pergamon Press.

Ford, D. H. and Urban, H. B.
1963 *Systems of Psychotherapy: A Comparative Study*. New York: John Wiley.

Frankl, V. E.
1955 *From Death Camp to Existentialism*, trans. L. Lasch. Boston: Beacon Press.

Gelatt, H. B.
1962 "Decision-Making: A Conceptual Frame of Reference for Counseling." *Journal of Counseling Psychology*, 9:240–245.

Hamachek, D. E.
1965 *The Self in Growth, Teaching, and Learning*. Englewood Cliffs, N.J.: Prentice-Hall.

Hobbs, N.
1962 "Sources of Gain in Psychotherapy." *American Psychologist*, 17:18–34.

Hosford, R.
   1969   "Behavioral Counseling: A Contemporary Overview." *The Counseling Psychologist,* 4:1–33.

Krumboltz, J. D.
   1966   "Behavioral Goals for Counseling." *Journal of Counseling Psychology,* 13:153–159.

Krumboltz, J. D. and Thoresen, C. E., eds.
   1969   *Behavioral Counseling.* New York: Holt, Rinehart and Winston.

Monstakas, C. E.
   1959   *Psychotherapy with Children.* New York: Harper and Row.

Patterson, C. H.
   1966   *Theories of Counseling and Psychotherapy.* New York: Harper and Row.

Paul, G.
   1966   *Insight vs. Desensitization in Psychotherapy.* Stanford, Calif.: Stanford University Press.

Ryan, T. A.
   1969   "Systems Techniques for Programs of Counseling and Counselor Education." *Educational Technology,* 9:7–17.

Salta, A.
   1961   *Conditioned Reflex Therapy: The Direct Approach to the Reconstruction of Personality.* New York: G. P. Putnam.

Thoresen, C. E.
   1969   "The Systems Approach and Counselor Education: Basic Features and Implications." *Counselor Education and Supervision,* 9:3–17.

Thoresen, C. and Mehrens, W. A.
   1967   "Decision Theory and Vocational Counseling: Important Concepts and Questions." *Personnel and Guidance Journal,* 46:165–172.

Ullmann, L. and Krasner, L.
   1965   *Case Studies in Behavior Modification.* New York: Holt, Rinehart and Winston.

Wolpe, J.
   1958   *Psychotherapy by Reciprocal Inhibition.* London: Oxford University Press.

Wolpe, J. and Lazarus, A. A.
   1966   *Behavior Therapy Techniques: A Guide to the Treatment of Neuroses.* London: Pergamon Press.

Chapter 7   Termination and Follow-Up

This chapter deals with the termination and follow-up of the counseling process and the use of each counseling procedure and technique. The process began in the initial session where the counselor worked toward creating an atmosphere in which the client felt at ease in saying the things he wanted to say. The second step was the establishment of a facilitative relationship characterized by empathic understanding, warmth, genuineness, and professionalism. This stage was followed by the client's identification of that area in which the counselor could be of some assistance, and the counselor's determination of how he could best help the client. This help, or the use of the most appropriate counseling procedure, was discussed in the previous chapter.

TERMINATION AND FOLLOW-UP OF THE COUNSELING STRATEGY When the counselor ceases to employ a counseling procedure, it can be said that he terminates the use of that procedure. He may terminate this use because it has been successful or unsuccessful in helping the client reach his goal. In order to evaluate its success, the counselor "follows-up" or seeks evaluation from the client or significant others in the client's life, such as a parent, teacher, or spouse. Based on this evaluation, the counselor may (1) decide to use another procedure if the first proved unsuccessful; (2) if successful, help the client to reformulate another specific goal for continuing counseling and begin again at the goal identification stage of the counseling process; or (3) if successful, and no other goal seems important or appropriate at this time, to terminate the counseling process.

TERMINATION AND FOLLOW-UP OF THE COUNSELING PROCESS When the counselor and client no longer see each other for the express purpose of counseling, the counseling process is terminated. It is the counselor's responsibility to evaluate the success that counseling has had for the client. This evaluation is made through "following-up" the client to determine if the goal reached as a result of counseling has stabilized over time. If it hasn't, such contact may lead to further counseling. This follow-up procedure is an integral, though removed, part of the complete counseling process.

COUNSELOR TERMINATING BEHAVIOR The goals of the terminating session are three: (1) to reinforce the client's behavior changes in the direction of the goal as stated by the client; (2) to make sure the client has no other pressing concerns; and (3) to help the client realize that he may seek the counselor's aid at any time in the future, as the "door is always open."

TERMINATION AS PART OF THE COUNSELING PROCESS There are some important emotions for both the client and the counselor in the termination stage. The counselor must be especially attuned to these emotions and be prepared to respond to them. To a great degree, the kinds of emotions which are likely to occur depend upon where the counseling process has gone and how successful counseling has been in achieving the outcome goals established in stage three, the identification of goals. The following approaches are the basic kinds of situations and the particular emotions associated with these situations.

Premature Termination Chosen by the Counselor   At times, external events in the counseling situation may require that counseling be terminated before successful goal attainment has occurred. This happens frequently in school situations: the end of the academic year may have occurred, the client may be moving to a new school, or the counselor may be leaving. These occurrences may not represent a serious difficulty if a close relationship has not as yet been established. But once a strong relationship has been established, premature termination may generate intense client feelings. This may occur where client and counselor have learned to trust each other deeply, to the point where the client has talked about many private and potentially embarrassing things: his sense of pervasive self-doubt, things about which he feels guilty, or things which could get him into trouble if significant others knew about them.

Clearly, the news of termination of counseling will have a strong emotional impact on the client. The client may feel betrayed by the counselor and angry toward him. The impact of counseling to this point may have been strong in the sense that the counselor has "opened up" the client but has not as yet helped him learn to accept and cope with his new awareness. The client most likely would feel frightened. He may well ask himself whether the counseling has been more harmful than helpful. It is possible that the client will blame the counselor for this difficult situation. After all, it is the counselor who is responsible for not only causing the painful awareness, but for prematurely terminating the relationship. Under such conditions, it would be a rare person who would not consider himself betrayed.

Any of these feelings, or combination of these, may be expected, and they are likely to be intense. They will not "go away." Counselor and client must deal with them together. The counselor himself may feel guilty about the impact he has had on his client and this may interfere with his ability to help the client deal effectively with his feelings. Since the feelings the client has toward the counselor are intense and negative, they may be threatening to the counselor. He may, thus, prefer to avoid looking at the client's feelings.

Clearly, this avoidance strategy would be the least appropriate and a most maladaptive alternative for the client's best interest. The client's feelings must be dealt with and the counselor must be the one to initiate it. For the counselor to do so will require a strong feeling of personal security. An insecure counselor could not possibly help the client discuss his negative feelings toward him.

The process of dealing with client feelings toward a counselor is basically the same as the process of dealing with client feelings at any stage of the counseling process. They must be dealt with openly and candidly by both parties and they must be accepted by the counselor in a non-evaluative and non-defensive manner. It will help considerably for the counselor to communicate his own feelings about the situation to the client saying, "I don't like what has happened either and I, too, wish this weren't the case. I understand your feelings very well, and although it hurts, I am glad you told me how you feel," may well offer strong support to the client. It may help, too, for the counselor to express his feelings about losing his relationship with the client: "I want you to know that I, too, feel hurt by this. Our relationship has meant a lot to me, and I, too, feel very badly that it must end soon. I feel badly that I have had to be the one to end it before it should be ended."

If the counselor had known before counseling began that he would be leaving, it would have been preferable to have avoided the awareness-oriented strategy, or else had communicated to the client in advance that he would be leaving soon. Thus, the news of the counselor's leaving would not be a surprise and both would have been prepared. The discussion here, however, assumes that the counselor did not know in advance that he would be leaving.

Under such conditions, an appropriate strategy might be to explore the possibility that another counselor can continue with the client. In choosing such a strategy, the counselor must be especially sensitive to the client's feelings of anger and betrayal. To such a proposal from the counselor, the client may respond with strong resistance. He may respond by saying, "Why go through it all again. I trusted you and had a strong relationship with you. I really don't believe I could accomplish that with someone else. It's too painful to have a deep relationship like we had and then lose it. I don't want to go through it again with someone else. Besides, what if he were to leave me too? That would be just another betrayal."

This is frequently the client's initial reaction. However, by the next session, some clients reconsider and choose to continue with a new counselor. If the counselor is to make a referral, he must be prepared to assure the client that the new counselor will also be competent, and this means the counselor himself must see the new counselor as competent to work with the client.

If the client chooses not to continue with a new counselor, the counselor must accept that decision. An exception to accepting the client's decision might be if the counselor sincerely believes that the client's future functioning would be severely impaired by leaving the client at the time of termination. However, since counselors value the concept of being aware of the consequences of alternatives, the counselor has an obligation to help the client understand the potential consequences of his choice. This is not the same as persuasion. It is one thing to help a person be aware of the consequences of the choice he has made, and another thing to *persuade* him to prefer another alternative.

Premature termination due to external involvements of the counselor has been considered intensively because it has some important implications for other stages of the counseling process. The crux of the problem is the client's intense negative feelings toward the counselor. The situation is just one clear example of a client who experiences strong negative feelings toward the counselor. Other experiences might include: a confrontation by the counselor; influencing the client to consider things he would rather avoid looking at; a time when the client believes nothing valuable is happening. The basic point to be made is that whenever something happens in the counseling process which influence the client's feelings toward the counselor, dealing openly with the new feelings has very high priority as an immediate process goal. This principle holds whether the new feelings are negative or positive. Frequently, the counselor must take the initiative to open the issue. When the feelings of the client are negative, the counselor must accept them without hostility or defensiveness. The feelings are the client's and he has a right to them.

The first of two basic strategies to be used in this situation is to help the client explore his feelings and come to some conclusion as to whether they are appropriate. A second is to explore the conditions of the counseling process (including, especially, the counselor's behavior) which influenced the feelings, asking whether it is possible to change the conditions or not. One must be careful here, for often the client's expression of anger toward the counselor is a manipulative ploy to control the counselor's actions. A crucial issue to consider is whether it is good or not good for a particular client to be able to manipulate the counselor. For some clients, having certain difficulties, being able to manipulate the counselor may have immediate favorable impact.

Premature Termination Chosen by the Client   Another especially critical situation in the counseling process occurs when the client communicates to the counselor that he has rejected the counselor as a viable source of help. This may occur at any stage of counseling. A client, especially a silent client, will communicate this from the very beginning of counseling. Another client may communicate rejection of the counselor later. One may communicate rejection simply by not returning for later sessions. Another might tell the counselor that he feels counseling is not valuable and worthwhile to him and he sees no point in continuing. Sometimes such a statement by a client will be quite appropriate. Counseling is not being of benefit to him. At other times, especially when counseling is awareness-based, such a response may suggest that the client is fearful about the impact counseling may have on him.

A major first step under such conditions is for the counselor to identify his own feelings about being rejected by his client. Fear and anger directed toward the client are likely counselor emotional responses under such conditions. Counselor-trainees are especially likely to respond with anxiety, for being rejected by the client is evaluated as reflecting counselor ineffectiveness. The counselor's goal is to be successful with his client. Being told that counseling is not being helpful may represent a serious block to goal attainment, a frustrating situation in which both anxiety and anger are likely responses.

Unfortunately, such emotional responses often interfere with effective counseling. Again, the general principle holds: when stress occurs in the relationship between the client and counselor, it is generally more adaptive to deal openly with the stress than to avoid dealing with it; responding to the stress in the relationship is far more likely to result in favorable consequences than will the avoidance of the stress.

Take as an example an adolescent female who has been seen three times for counseling. At the beginning of the fourth session, she says, "I've been thinking it over and I've pretty well decided that counseling is not doing me any good. Nothing has changed and it doesn't look like anything will. You're a nice person and I don't want to make you feel bad, but counseling has really been a waste of time for me."

Such a client response is likely to make the counselor feel anxious, angry, and, possibly, guilty. The client has challenged the counselor's competency and security. Any counselor not aware of the emotional impact of this client's response would be unlikely to respond effectively at this point.

Borrowing from the basic principle, an effective counselor strategy would appear to be to discuss openly what is involved in the client's decision. The following response would appear highly adaptive in facilitating this process goal: "You've certainly made it clear that you don't see counseling as being worthwhile for you. First, I want you to know that although what you have told me upsets me, nonetheless, I am glad you did tell me this. Could you tell me how you came to this conclusion?"

> *Client:* As I said, nothing seems to be changing. Nothing new has happened. We seem to be going 'round and 'round in circles and never getting anywhere. . . . I don't feel we're getting anywhere with my problem.
>
> *Counselor:* I guess this counseling experience has been quite frustrating for you and that

you are giving up hope that anything valuable could happen. . . . Could you tell me what you think should be happening here for counseling to be worthwhile for you?

Client: Well, like we seem to be trying to understand me—my attitudes toward myself, my parents, teachers, and school, and all like that. Well, you know, that's been interesting and all, but it hasn't helped me with my anxiousness when I take tests. Like I took another test just last week. I knew the stuff, but I froze up and failed it just like the others.

Note that at this point the counselor chose to deal with the issue openly. He responded first to his own feelings and then commenced to explore the issue of what should be, but was not, happening. Alternative counselor responses to the client's opening lead might have been, "Well, I guess it's your privilege to decide against further counseling. I wish it could have worked out more favorably for you." Or, "You said counseling has been a real waste of time for you, and that nothing has changed. But I really wonder if that is so? Do you *really* feel that *nothing* has changed?" From this case, try to think through the impact each of these response leads would have for the counseling process.

Critical situations like the one given above *force* the counselor to make serious and important decisions. He must decide whether the client's criticisms that nothing valuable or instrumental to the attainment of outcome goals are valid, or whether they represent "defensive ploys." If he decides the criticisms are valid, he must reassess and reevaluate his intervention strategy. In intensive counseling, the counselor must always evaluate and reevaluate the appropriateness and efficacy of his intervention strategy. Where it is not paying off, he must be willing to modify his strategy and perhaps even choose a completely new one. In the above example, the goal of counseling was to reduce test anxiety. That goal had been determined in earlier counseling sessions From the client's remarks, it was clear that the counselor's strategy was based on facilitating awareness. The feedback he received from the client was that this strategy was not paying off. The counselor must decide, then, whether persisting with that strategy would eventually pay off, or whether implementing a new strategy would be more likely to achieve the goal of reducing test anxiety. Using systematic desensitization is a very different strategy, which, for this counseling goal, would appear to have a higher likelihood of success.

Termination as a Consequence of Successful Counseling   In the goal-setting stage, the client and counselor determine counseling goals and establish criteria for determining when these goals could be considered attained. In the termination stage, they must consider the criteria, assess the changes that have occurred, and, on this basis, evaluate whether counseling has been successful. If it has been successful, the client's behavior outside the counselor's office must have changed and the new behaviors must be value judged as more desirable than the old behaviors. Even in similar cases where counseling has been successful, some important emotions may occur which must be dealt with.

One of the bases of the kind of intensive counseling described here is the relationship between client and counselor. For counseling to be of maximum impact, the relationship must be uncommonly close and intense. When counseling goals have been attained, it is time for the intense relationship to be terminated. As anyone who has experienced the separation of a loved one can attest, terminating an intense relationship is not easy for anyone involved. The last few moments of the relationship can frequently be the most difficult.

There is a natural tendency to feel a sense of loss, a void, a feeling of loneliness when an intense relationship is to be terminated. Once again, the counselor cannot deal with these feelings by avoiding them. He must handle the termination process so that the client feels he can be independent of the counselor.

Probably the easiest strategy is to review and summarize what has happened—the stages of counseling, and the kinds of changes that have occurred. Once accomplished, it is highly appropriate for the counselor to communicate the impact the counseling experience has had on him and how he has felt toward the client. This makes it easier for the client to share his feelings, and if appropriate, express his gratitude. Once this has occurred, formal termination is usually easier.

Frequently, clients feel unsure about whether they are ready to terminate. They have seen things change through counseling, but they have always felt that when things went badly they could turn to the counselor for help and support. When termination occurs, the counselor will no longer be available. If the counselor senses such insecurity, it must be discussed before termination can be completed. Of course, it would be wise to anticipate this difficulty and work it through several sessions prior to termination, but such is not always possible. An appropriate counselor response lead to enter into this area might be, "We certainly have achieved some important changes since we have been together. In fact, it looks as though we have pretty well achieved what we set out to accomplish. Sometimes people who have changed a lot wonder whether they are really ready to handle situations, especially difficult and new situations, that they may encounter. I wonder if you might feel that way?"

If the client answers, "No," and the counselor accepts his answer as valid, things are fine. If the client says, "Yes," then the insecurity must be explored. If there are situations which both the client and counselor would agree would be difficult for the client to handle, then termination would be premature. If the client says, "I am not sure," and on further discussion he experiences the normal anxiety of entering into a new situation, then the counselor can help the client reassure himself by recalling the previous "new situations" that he has handled so effectively.

An important dimension which emerges from this discussion is that of client dependency on the counselor. Counselors generally believe that it is good and desirable for their clients to be self-reliant—not dependent on others to attain goals that are important to them. However, the issue is considerably more complex. The mere fact that clients seek a counselor's help suggests that in some way client dependence on the counselor is an inherent and unavoidable part of the counseling process. By coming to the counselor for help, the client implies that he is dependent on the counselor for help to deal with whatever concerns he wishes to discuss. When goals of counseling are established, it is clear that the client is dependent on the counselor to help him attain those goals. By continuing in counseling, the client implies that he believes he has a better chance of attaining his counseling-related goals with the counselor's help than without it—clearly a statement of implicit dependency.

There are some important responsibilities associated with being a person on whom another is dependent. One ethical responsibility is that the counselor may not use the client's dependence for his own benefit. This is an especially important principle for counselors who enjoy having others dependent upon them ("mother" or "father" figures).

A second responsibility is to determine the "limits of dependence." It is one thing for a client to be dependent on a counselor for help in attaining goals of counseling; it is another for the client to be dependent on the counselor as a source of human caring and interest. Clearly, if perpetuated, the latter would not be in the best interest of either client or counselor. Nor is it in the best interest of the client for him to seek approval and support from the counselor for every action he undertakes. Eventually, the client must decide on what actions are best for him without the counselor's approval. This goal must be attained before counseling can be effectively terminated.

A third area of responsibility is that after the stated goals of counseling are attained, the counselor must help the client learn to use the new behaviors and skills to cope with new situations on his own, without the counselor's help. The counseling relationship, however intense, is always temporary. When it is terminated, it is generally best for all parties involved to terminate it as fully as possible. This means that at the end of the counseling relationship, the client must be able to function on his own without being dependent upon the counselor for further help.

CRITERIA FOR DETERMINING SUCCESS Borrowing from the notions of Chapter 5, in order to evaluate whether counseling has been successful or not, criteria for success must be established. If counseling has been successful, then some change in behavior must have occurred. Thus establishing criteria for success includes identifying the new behaviors which are to occur and the conditions or situations in which such behaviors are to occur. Below are adequately stated criteria for determining counseling success for each of five clients.

The first client came to the counselor and indicated that when she takes tests she freezes, becomes "up tight," and usually "blows" the tests. The second client reported he just could not seem to make friends. The third client was referred to the counselor by one of his teachers. The teacher indicated that this client starts trouble by causing fights and other disruptions. The fourth client, an adult, came on his own and described himself as a "wishy-washy" person who was afraid to say anything, at any time, and anywhere. The fifth client stated that he had a poor self-image and no self-confidence.

During the goal-setting stage, criteria for determining counseling success were established for each of the five clients. They are stated as follows:

Client 1: Counseling will be successful when the client takes tests and reports that whatever anxiety is experienced is controllable and does not interfere with her effective performance on tests.

Client 2: Counseling will be successful when the client interacts with his peers on the playground and after school, and reports that the group has accepted him as an equal.

Client 3: Counseling will be successful when three consecutive weeks have passed with not one fighting incident reported by the client or a member of the school faculty.

Client 4: Counseling will be successful when the client demonstrates that he can assert his position strongly and forcefully on debatable issues, and will be able to demonstrate this when a position contrary to his is taken by a significant other.

Client 5: Counseling will be successful when the client stops saying to himself that he is worthless and incompetent even when his performance does not meet his own standards of acceptability.

Note that in all cases the new, more desirable behavior and the situations in which that desirable behavior should occur are clearly specified. For each client counseling would be successful when his respective criteria are considered attained. During the termination stage client and counselor mutually consider the criteria established during the goal-setting stage and evaluate whether these goals have been attained. The primary purpose of the termination stage, then, is to determine whether counseling has been successful. Another essential goal is that of working through the emotional investment associated with the intensely close relationship maintained throughout the counseling process.

CASE OF DOREEN This client was a thirty-six-year-old married woman who sought counseling because of several difficulties she was having with handling her own emotions and her relationship with her husband and her three stepchildren. The goals set up in counseling focused on her intrapersonal difficulties. When upset, Doreen would have severe headaches and lock herself in her room for days at a time. The following is a typescript of the eighth and final session of counseling. This typescript demonstrates the termination procedure as discussed in this chapter.

Client 1:	You can ask me how I am—I'm fine, I'm smart.
Counselor 1:	How are you?
Client 2:	I'm fine. I can control myself.
Counselor 2:	I'm glad.
Client 3:	I have problems but they're not way big as they used to be. I lost my temper only one time.
Counselor 3:	In two weeks . . . ?
Client 4:	Yeh. . . .
Counselor 4:	Wonderful.

Client 5:   Yes. I mean—like usual I couldn't find anything to break so I picked up my house slipper and threw it against the wall. My husband, he won't give me a chance to break anything. [*Laughing*] He gets all scared. I was picking things up and throwing them and then he gets all shook up; he started picking things up and throwing them. And I said, "Gee, I'm glad I'm helping you." And we both laughed cause it was so funny. But, it made me feel . . . you know. . . . But, he still doesn't understand it . . . but I want to, uh . . . I mean it makes me feel better if. . . .

Counselor 5:   [*Interrupting*] Right! To get it out. Sure.

Client 6:   He gets all shook up, because he doesn't see me like that, you know. . . . Well, he's never, I. . . . It's just been lately I've been doing that. . . .

Counselor 6:   That's good. And you're feeling better for it. Headaches? Any headaches?

Client 7:   Well, just that . . . like, I say that one time. . . . But now, maybe I have a headache and I don't even know. It's uh . . . one of the twins . . . he and I are so good friends it's pitiful. And he wants to be with me all the time; he's in the kitchen with me and . . . last night, I was so shocked, I was laying in bed watching TV 'cause my husband wanted another show and I wanted another one. So I stayed in my room. . . . And Billy just walked in and lay on the bed with me. I mean, I didn't say one word; but . . . and then he was really enjoying it. And I was shocked. I mean, you know. . . . Then he said, you know, "I wish I could stay up later," and I didn't say anything. So he said, "Well, goodnight, Mommy." I mean, but, we're friends. We're having a real big problem with the other one. Well, I don't know if my husband should; but now when I tell my husband, gee, he did this today again. What am I going to do? He says, "Well, you know, he's . . . what he's doing, you cannot blame him for it, because he's sick . . . or something." Well, I . . . I don't know. But now Steve's stealing in school and, I mean, my children are all embarrassed. . . . They've had money missing in school and I know it's Steve, because he's brought the money home and. . . . He's been buying milk wnen we haven't given him any money to buy milk. And . . . . So. . . . I don't know. And then, Bill comes home and says, "Mommy, I'm so ashamed because Steve took some money." But since Bill had done it before. Remember, I told you . . . that happened? They went and got Bill and questioned him. This lady saw the boy, and she said it was Bill. But she didn't know we had twins. So, Bill is so hurt. You know, he said, "You know teachers scold me because . . . ." And he told her that, "No, it's my brother. Not me." And then my other son got embarrassed because he said everybody's talking about Billy stole some money because Bill's name is Bill, and Billy's name is Willy. [*Laughing*] I mean, the whole family's all messed up in school because of that.

Counselor 7: But, you're doing a lot. . . .

Client 8: Oh, yes. Yes. But like I said I . . . worry about the children, so. . . . But, it's not as bad as it used to be. I mean . . . uh, I keep thinking, well, Steve's going to get hell, but. . . . I mean, he won't talk. I . . . I can be mean to him; he won't buy that. I can be real nice to him. . . . He'll just say, "I don't know, I don't know." And twice already, I asked him, I says, "Steve, please tell me how much you took so I can pay back the money. Mommy and Daddy are so embarrassed, but we want to pay the kids back that you. . . ." He said, "I told you I don't know!" And he just walks away, you know. So I told my husband, "You know, I give up. I mean, what am I gonna do?" But it . . . bothers me. I mean, uh . . . and he keeps saying, "I wish . . . I can't wait till we go to grandma's." So, she's the only one, you know. . . . 'Cause when we see her, first thing he does is cry. Then he tells her his troubles.

And us . . . Bill's not enjoying counseling too much. He says, "Well. . . ." One week . . . the other week he came home happy. I said, "Oh! You know you had a nice time?" He said, "Yeh, we didn't have anything to talk about, so we played." So then this Monday came, he said, "Oh, we're going. . . ." He's happy at going. He came home, y'know, so I said, "What's happened, Bill?" He said, "Nothing." He went upstairs. So when he came down to my room, I said, "Bill, what happened Monday with the counselor?" He said, "Oh, we talked for ten minutes. . . ." I told him, "Tell him *anything* you want to." He said, "Yeh, but only ten minutes we talked, and I don't know what to talk about, so we just sat there." And he said he just sat for the rest of the time. And he came home mad. Oh, he was mad. [*Laughing*] He said, "I don't like this kind."

But, Steve, he comes home, like nothing happened, or . . . like he just went for a ride and came home. I worry because I keep wishing I knew what was going on in his mind. If he would just say, "Okay, I stole the money." 'Cause we didn't beat him up or anything. We just want to make everything right and help him. And he goes to school and he takes his clothes off. I mean, he unbuttons all his shirt and. . . . He's acting cuckoo in school, the kids come home and tell me. So my husband said, "Gee, we don't know. . . ." I mean, do you think I should tell the teacher . . . uh . . . that he's going to counseling, or us . . . ?

Counselor 8: Why don't you wait and see what happens in counseling.

Client 9: I mean, the teacher called me, and she said, "Any help she can give." You know. And . . . but, I don't want her to do something else . . . and, you know, would be different from his counselor. Then we'd really kind of mix him up. But as far as me, I'm just fine. I mean, um.

Counselor 9:   I'm glad.

Client 10:   I did yesterday what I wouldn't do in my whole life. I mean, uh . . . oh, I don't know. In a way I think I hurt somebody's feelings without being rude, or something like that. Well, my daughter had brought some pizza home for a class, for me to hold . . . in our freezer. And I keep telling her, "Y'know, I gotta go shopping. So, we have no room. It's just a small little thing; but . . . you kids are going to have a party. Okay, I help you." So three Saturdays went by and nobody picked those pizzas up and . . . I been putting my meat someplace else. . . . So I told Sharen, "Do something about it." She says, "Oh, the kids said just hold it." So what I did was I wrote a little note to the teacher and I sent Willy with the pizzas. The boy just picked up the pizzas and found a place for them. But I told the teacher I was sorry. I didn't want to do this and hurt the kids. But if I keep it any longer, I think they'll only take advantage of it. And it made me feel real good. And when Sharen came home, I said, "Ooo, anybody mad at me?" And she said, "Oh, no. No, nothing. . . ." So, well, I never did that before. I would hold it and hold it. But I thought I'll try this once. I mean, you know . . . well . . . so it made me feel real good. . . . I don't know, it's just like I been coming to school. Something . . . to a class . . . I mean I learn, uh . . . you know, to . . . well . . . anyway, it's helped.

Counselor 10: Is there anything else I can help you with?

Client 11: No. I don't think so. Because like I said, because myself . . . I feel fine. It's just that I'm worried about the children. But I can't come here for them.

Counselor 11: That's right.

Client 12: Gee, I said it, that's their problem, huh? [*Laughs*]

Counselor 12: That's right. [*Laughs*]

Client 13: Oh boy. [*Laughs*]

Counselor 13: Yep. [*Laughs*]

Client 14: I mean I want to help, but. . . .

Counselor 14: Are . . . uh . . . any of the counselors seeing your husband?

Client 15: Only one. Only Steve's, but my husband, see, writes down, y'know all week what Steve does . . . anything unusual, and then he tells her. I don't know if it helps, but . . . like you said, you know when he does something good . . . uh . . . praise him and all that?

Counselor 15: Yes.

Client 16: Doesn't do anything good. I mean all he does is go to bed on time. Which we tell him is good and all that kind. But that's all he does. The rest of the time he's rude. He's like a big bully and no respect. And he . . . he won't put his clothes in the wash yet. [*Laughs*] And he'll go to school with the same clothes and . . . so my husband said, "Well, if it makes you. . . ." Well, twice I've gone I'll go get his clothes, but . . . after that I thought, well, heck, that's too bad and I'm getting tired of, you know. So then, now, the kids are . . . I don't know, whether the kids are trying to help me, or what? But when Steve sits next to them, they all move.

Counselor 16: Um, hmm.

Client 17: And they did that to him, oh, one night. Everybody moved. So I said, "What's a matter?" and they said, "Oh, Steve's pajamas smell." So when I went . . . that night, I was surprised, the pajamas were in that basket, the laundry basket. So I said, "See, the kids are catching on then." And now the children, any time they're mad, they just ignore each other. Y'know, they even ignore me or my husband [*Laughs*] but that's all right with us. But my husband. I . . . I don't know, I think maybe if my husband did, you know, come like this, he'd understand more. Things seem to bother him a lot now. I mean, when I tell him, "Well, that doesn't bother me," he says, "Well, it should. It bothers me!" [*Laughs*]

Counselor 17: [*Laughs*]

Client 18: I mean, I'm surprised that I . . . lots of things that I don't feel; it's bothering him.

Counselor 18: Uh, huh.

Client 19: So I told him in the car, "Why don't you go to counseling? Why don't you try?" He said, "Oh, I don't need it." So, but everything seems . . . I notice now . . . everything's bothering him.

Counselor 19: Yeh.

Client 20: I mean, uh, he feels hurt when the kids don't do something or say something. You know now he's feeling hurt because of my oldest daughter. She doesn't kiss him goodnight. And he

had a long talk. And she told him she
had reasons, but she didn't want to
tell him. So he's feeling hurt. So I told
him, "You know, it doesn't bother me
the kids don't kiss me goodnight, as
long as I know they love me and they
respect me and. . . ." But he said it
bothers him. He said because well,
affection means something. But like I
said, I'm Oriental . . . and, you know
we don't have that kind, so it doesn't
bother me.

Counselor 20: Right.

Client 21: I mean uh . . . but it's really bothering
him. And he told me, he said, "Well,
Billy kisses you goodnight." I said,
"Well, for a while he did because he
thought he had to, since I got married
to you."

Counselor 21: Oh, yeh.

Client 22: So Billy kisses me goodnight. Well, to
me it was okay, but yet, you know,
uh. . . . It didn't bother me if he did or
didn't. And he stopped. I think he was
kind of ashamed. You know how boys
are when they get to be 12. And I understand, but my husband doesn't.

Counselor 22: How are you handling the kinds of . . .
hate feelings that you have, Doreen?

Client 23: Well. . . . That's the only part Steve's doing; I hate him. But I don't want to hurt
him. But he, because I hate him, I
think of my mother-in-law and I hate
her more. I mean, my husband and I
argued about my mother-in-law two
nights now. He told me, us. . . . Well,
I told him . . . the way Steve is . . . and
just imagine what's going to happen

when we go there. So, I don't want to go.

Counselor 23:   Oh, yeh.

Client 24:   So my husband. . . .

Counselor 24:   [*Interrupting*] That's pretty soon, isn't it?

Client 25:   Yeh. After school. I mean, on vacation. So I told him, "I don't want to go, be-cause, well, I don't know." I told him. I learn so much and now I can control myself and maybe I'll just tell her, you know, "Be quiet," or tell her to mind her business, or something. My hus-band doesn't want me to.

Counselor 25:   Yeh.

Client 26:   He said, "Oh, well, can't you just take it for thirty-six hours?" I said, "Well, I don't know . . . the way I feel right now . . . I think I can tell her." And he's getting scared. So he said, "Well, can't you do this for hu . . . mani . . . tarian purpose?" What's that mean?

Counselor 26:   [*Laughs*] Just, uh . . . in terms of one human to another, you know.

Client 27:   Oh. That's what he told me. I said, "I don't know, whatever that means, I don't know." He said, that's what he said, "Can I do it for humanitarian purpose?"

Counselor 27:   You do whatever it is you'd like to do that'll make you feel better.

Client 28:   Well, what I was thinking. I don't want to go, yet I'll go, but . . . if I see Steve doing . . . you know, running to her and start crying and saying, "You know, Grandma, Mommy did. . . ." I want to tell her. Or I want to go up and say, "Steve, will you please leave her alone and get away." I never been able to say that, but uh. . . . But that's what he does. It's happened every time. As soon as he sees grandma, he, he starts crying.

Counselor 28: And unloads all his problems, troubles.

Client 29: And she believes him, she does. And my husband and I haven't told her anything about the boys going to counseling, or me, or anything, you know; my husband don't want me to. . . . So ·I told my husband, "If it gets worse, I'm going to tell her. Everything that's happening here." And all the letters I write, I kinda lie a little bit. Tell 'em how good the children are and all that, but . . . I guess that's for humanitarian purpose. No, but. . . . It's too bad. Steve seems to be getting worse than better. But I was just thinking. Well, it's just like me. For a while I was getting terrible. I mean a real upset and so maybe it's his turn to kinda mess it up a little bit. I'm hoping, you know.

Counselor 29: Yeh, I'm sure he's struggling; trying to find himself, you know. And this is uh . . . coming out in all kinds of ways.

Client 30: Well, I hope the counselor is having, you know, success with Steve. Because he don't talk. He just don't talk. I mean, at home they blah, blah, blah. But when we go out to people, they don't talk. Only Grandma, is the only time. And I tried to tell Bill, "Tell him. Tell the man." He said, "Well, what am I going to tell him?" I said, "Tell the man if you like school or if you ʲon't like your teachers." He said,

"Oh, I'm not. . . ." I said, "No, tell him anything. If you're mad at me, or if you're mad at daddy, or you know. . . . You tell him." But Bill doesn't understand. But, he says he doesn't like to talk. He said, "I don't like to talk. So we just sit." But he'll . . . he'll answer questions. But they won't just talk.

Counselor 30: Yeh . . . [*Pause*]

Client 31: But other than that. . . .

Counselor 31: It seems to me that uh. . . .

Client 32: Oh. And I met a boy from Purdue. He, my husband's cousin, came to visit and he brought a boy from Purdue. And we were talking. And then he brought uh . . . he's taking psychology.

Counselor 32: Oh, yeh.

Client 33: So then, uh. . . . And I just told him, "Oh! I know a psychologist!" He says, "You do?" He said, "Who?" and I said, "Oh, a Dr. ——," and he said, "Hey! I read some of his . . . !" I said, "He's the one!" "You know him?" I said, "Oh yeh." My husband, he looked at me. . . . [*Both laugh*] So this boy was telling me about, he went and got analyzed. You know.

Counselor 33: Oh, yeh.

Client 34: He had his problems, too, and I looked at him and I said, "I bet you I know what your problem is," and he says, "Oh." And then he went and got his handbag with all his junk. But he said he feels good, going and talking like that. So he's taking a course. And he said he read a lot of yours; they got at his school. All these papers and stuff.

Counselor 34: I figured [*Laughs*] it does.

Client 35: Well, that's good. Boy, I wish my husband would come.

Counselor 35: Well, if he . . . if he would ever like to . . . uh . . . all he has to do is call.

Client 36: Well, he won't. I mean, uh . . . maybe I can help him at home. [*Laughs*]

Counselor 36: Yeh. Well. [*Both talk together*]

Client 37: He always tells me I'm smart-alecky, because . . . just because, you know, I think I know uh. . . .

Counselor 37: Well, you do.

Client 38: Well, that's good. That means I don't have to see you anymore. [*Laughs*]

Counselor 38: Nope [*Laughs*] and that's good, huh? [*Both laugh*]

Client 39: But for the first time I have to tell someone it's so good not to to be able to fear anymore.

Counselor 39: I'm glad. [*Laughs*] I really am.

Client 40: [*Laughs*] I hope I never see you again. [*Both laugh*]

Counselor 40: Wonderful!

Client 41: Boy! That makes me feel good.

Counselor 41: Yeh.

Client 42: Now I can go out and lick the world. [*Laughs*]

Counselor 42: You can. You're one person that can. I mean that. [*Serious*]

Client 43: I don't know. It's just that I've learned to tell myself everytime I do something, or I get upset. I tell myself, "Oh, you're doing it." And my husband reminds me all the time, too, that I'm upsetting myself. 'Cause sometimes I get mad and I say, "Oh, just because of Steve." And he says, "No, just because of you." Which is true. Well, that's good then. I'll go home and let you go home. [*Laughs*]

Counselor 43:   Well . . . yeh, if anything were to happen, although I don't think it will, if it would, just give me a call.

Client 44:   Oh. Thank you. [*Laughs*]

Counselor 44:   I'm always here. And it's been very nice talking to you and I've enjoyed it very much.

Client 45:   Like I said it's like coming to school. I found out a lot about myself. I'm not ugly. I'm not mean. I'm not [*Laughs*] . . . I'm terrific.

Counselor 45:   That's right. You sure are.

Client 46:   Thank you. Bye, bye.

Counselor 46:   Goodbye.

Client 47:   I hope I never have to see you again.

SUGGESTIONS FOR
FURTHER READING

Eysenck, H. J.
   1965   "The Effects of Psychotherapy." *International Journal of Psychiatry*, 1:99–144.

Hock, P. H. and Zubin, J., eds.
   1964   *The Evaluation of Psychiatric Treatment.* New York: Grune and Stratton.

Paul, G.
   1967   "Insight vs. Desensitization in Psychotherapy Two Years After Termination." *Journal of Consulting Psychology*, 31:333–348.

   1967   "Strategy of Outcome Research in Psychotherapy." *Journal of Counseling Psychology*, 31:109–118.

Ullmann, L. and Krasner, L.
   1965   *Case Studies in Behavior Modification.* New York: Holt, Rinehart and Winston.

Chapter 8   Summary Perspective

Counseling is a process by which a person is helped to behave in a more rewarding manner. Such assistance, as offered, is determined by the counselor; that which is more rewarding is determined by the person with the aid of the counselor. Individuals seek assistance from professional counselors for a variety of reasons— from the desire for help in making a simple decision to a desperate plea for relief from confusion, turmoil, fear, guilt, and excessive environmental pressures. It appears that the need for assistance is increasing in our society as evidenced by the waiting lists of agencies offering counseling services. As a result there is a need for counselors who can offer the most appropriate aid to the greatest number of people seeking help. This will necessitate a short-term counseling process model and an in-depth understanding of the important principles upon which this process is based.

The first principle is that all human behavior is purposive and goal directed. The counselor, in order to have maximum impact on the client, must accept the responsibility to behave in such ways as to facilitate client progress toward desired goals. The second principle is that in the process, more immediate goals must be attained before moving toward long-term goals. Third, the counselor must evaluate the impact he is having on the client in terms of the immediate and long-term goals. These goals are defined as client change toward desired behavior, and is the result of an effective counseling process.

The counselor in the *initial session,* the first time the counselor and client meet, has two primary objectives: (1) to create an atmosphere in which the client can feel free to say the things he wants to say, and (2) to help the client realize that the counselor is listening and understanding what the client is saying. Counselor behavior includes: the modeling of a state of relaxation for the client; listening-attentive behaviors; understanding the feedback of client responses; and motivation of the client for counseling. A counselor behavior basic to all of these is the reflective response lead used to help the client orient his thinking. By "reflecting" back to the client what he has been saying, the counselor influences, by his responses, the direction, content, and nature of future dialogue.

If the client feels comfortable and safe with the counselor, then he is more likely to speak about himself and the world in which he lives. These conditions are absolutely necessary if the client is to gain anything from his encounters with the counselor.

The *second stage* in the counseling process is the development and maintenance of a facilitative relationship. The components of this relationship include: empathic understanding; warmth and acceptance; genuineness and honesty; and professional competence. To have empathic understanding, the counselor must know how the client feels and what the client is experiencing. The counselor communicates warmth and acceptance not only by response leads, but also by his voice tones and nonverbal cues, as facial expressions. In order for a counselor to be honest and genuine with a client, he must first be aware of his own values and beliefs in the counseling situation. The extent of a counselor's impact with his client is directly related to his ability and willingness to be can did with him. Implicit in the conditions necessary for a facilitative relationship is the professional competency of the counselor. Frequently, the difference between whether clients change or not as a result of counseling is whether or not they are hopeful and confident that the counselor has the competency to help them improve.

The establishment of the facilitative relationship is purposive and goal directed, not as an objective in itself, but as a stage in the counseling process. The relationship is established in order to facilitate the counselor's evaluation of: (1) what it is that the client wants to get out of the counseling process; (2) what it is that is motivating the client to seek assistance in light of what it is he desires to change; (3) what counselor strategies are more relevant to the client and his situation in helping him to change; and (4) what new learnings must be mastered by the client in order to insure the success of new behavior as it is related to his goal in the process.

Counselor goal identification behaviors and determination of the counseling strategies characterize the *third stage* of the counseling process. This stage has four important and interrelated components: (1) the establishment of target or outcome goals of counseling; (2) the determination and consideration of client characteristics which might influence the counselor's strategy; (3) the thinking through of those process goals which must be attained if later outcome goals are to be attained and the sequence in which those process goals might occur; and (4) the development of a strategy (or plan of action) to be implemented to help the client achieve the identified goal.

Counseling can be described as successful when some kind of change of desirable, observable behavior has occurred. In order to determine what is desirable behavior and how to evaluate the change in behavior, it is essential to identify the target or goal of the counseling process in as specific a manner as possible. The manner in which the counselor responds to his client is functionally related to the successful attainment of the goal. A counselor verbal response, which is especially instrumental during the goal-setting stage, is the Counselor Tacting Response Lead (CTRL). This response lead, essential to establishing goals, is categorized as follows: (1) CTRLs aid both the counselor and the client to operationally define the terms the client is using (e.g., "Tell me what you mean when you say that you are nervous"); (2) CTRLs aid both the client and the counselor to experience vicariously the significant happenings and circumstances that surround some specific event (e.g., "Tell me about a time when you felt particularly nervous"); (3) CTRLs aid both the client and the counselor to vicariously experience any physiological reaction and change at the time of the specific experience (e.g. "Tell me how you felt physically in the situation in which you were particularly nervous"); and (4) by the continued use of CTRLs, the client will be able to respond with specific situations, feelings, and physical reactions to props in his environment. All of these counselor impact behaviors are to aid the client to identify what it is he is seeking as a result of counseling. What is sought by the client must be able to be stated as a specific change in his behavior or pattern of behaving.

Following goal identification, the counselor must assess, both physically and psychologically, the client's ability to behave in the desired manner. The behavior, itself, must be within the client's class and range of behavior. Referral of the client for a physical assessment to a physician is essential if the counselor believes there is an incapacity which might hinder the client's development toward the desired goal. Psychological assessment includes: level of intellectual functioning and development, emotional state, self-concept, interpersonal relationship characteristics, client expectations, and personality construct dimensions. After client psychophysical assessment, the counselor has the responsibility to map a strategy to facilitate client growth and development toward the identified goal. This requires the counselor's consent and confidence that the identified goal is worthwhile for the client and that the goal is realistic and can be achieved.

The term "strategy" is used to refer to the planning process of counseling, the planning activity of the counselor in his consideration of the goals of counseling, the characteristics of the client, and the process goals which must be attained if outcome goals are to be achieved. The counselor's impact is directly related to his ability to systematically apply principles based on human behavior acquisition and its change. Once a strategy is decided upon, the client must be educated in the use of the strategy, followed by his consent and commitment in the use of the strategy. This commitment may be termed a verbal contract between counselor and client. The actual use of the counseling strategy comprises the *fourth stage* in the counseling process.

Some people learn new behaviors by receiving verbal instructions from significant others. Based upon this principle, and operationally using it, several strategies have been developed for counselor use (Chapter 6): (1) systematic desensitization, to reduce or eliminate undesirable and maladaptive anxiety responses by replacing these responses with relaxation responses considered incompatible with the anxiety responses; (2) paradoxical intention, using the assumption that fear makes what is feared come true and that positively portraying the symptoms of fear makes what is feared appear ridiculous; (3) direct instruction, used to help a client think (and, therefore, behave) in a more reasonable and rational manner; (4) bibliotherapy, an instructional technique using textual material to help some clients gain a better understanding of their problem; (5) thought interference, the inhibiting of thought processes that lead to client maladaptive behavior; (6) assertive training, the reduction of inhibition by the practice of responses that reduce anxiety; and (7) aversion training, the process of increasing anxiety toward a particular stimulus in order to develop an aversion to that stimulus.

Another principle of human behavior is that some clients learn to behave in new ways by imitating and observing the behavior, beliefs, values, and attitudes of significant others. Clearly, a counselor may help his client to learn to function more effectively by identifying himself as a model who is likely to be emulated, and then behaving in those ways which he believes will be instrumental to the effective functioning of the client. Three specific approaches to the actual counselor application of this principle are: (1) role playing, used to enable the client to gain understanding of himself and of others in his environment, to determine how he may wish to modify his behavior, and to practice the modified behavior that he desires; (2) the maintenance of the counseling relationship based on the modeling procedure where the client has regard and respect for the counselor, so that the client would become more like the counselor; and (3) the use of media to present models, a procedure similar to that of bibliotherapy except that the material used is audio and/or video tapes, records, and films.

A third principle of human behavior, upon which counseling process strategies are based, is that the reinforcement contingencies in a person's environment influence the way he behaves in that environment. Changing the reinforcement contingencies can be expected to influence a change in behavior. The counseling techniques based upon this principle are: (1) operant conditioning, characterized by the counselor directly rewarding specific client behavior change; (2) successive approximation of goal, a step-by-step reward method of directing client behavior toward the desired goal; (3) positive attention, based on the reinforcement potential of positive attention, while ignoring all unwanted behaviors; (4) extinction through non-reinforcement, modifying a behavior by changing the reward structure so that it is no longer rewarding to behave in a certain manner; and (5) discrimination training, helping the client discriminate between two situations so that his behavior in one situation can no longer be applicable to a similar situation.

Some people learn to function more effectively by becoming aware of certain characteristics about themselves and their environment. Awareness, then, is a major process goal of counseling. For some clients, especially those needing to make career and/or educational decisions, awareness of specific skills, talents, aptitudes, and interests will be essential. For other clients, an awareness of emotions becomes essential. Helping a client become aware of the dominant emotions he tends to experience, the intensity of those emotions, and the situation in which these are likely to occur, may be an especially impactful awareness-based process goal.

In order to change behavior, some people need to learn the decision-making process. The methodology of this process as a counseling strategy is that of: identifying the problem, determining goals, describing existing conditions related to the problem, generating all potential alternatives, predicting the likelihood of possible consequences, value judging the desirability of all possible consequences of each alternative, selecting and implementing the alternative selection, and evaluating the actual consequences of this alternative behavior.

Lastly, some people learn to function more effectively by acquiring a more favorable sense of self-esteem. The image a person has of himself, the beliefs he maintains about himself, and his own sense of self-esteem are seen as factors which influence the effectiveness with which he functions. Thus, the counseling strategy of changing a client's concept of self from negative to positive is viewed as a relevant process goal for many clients, which if attained, will help them function more effectively.

Termination and follow-up, the *fifth and final stage* in the counseling process, refers to the counseling strategy as well as the process itself. In terminating the strategy, and following up on its effectiveness, the counselor must decide, (1) to use another strategy if the first proved unsuccessful; (2) to help the client to reformulate another specific goal for continuing counseling, if the strategy was successful; or (3) if successful, and no other goal seems important or appropriate at that time, to terminate the counseling process. In terminating the process, whether this decision is prematurely chosen by the counselor or client, or as a consequence of successful counseling, the counselor should behave in a manner, (1) to reinforce the client's behavior changes in the direction of the desired goal; (2) to make sure the client has no other pressing concerns; and (3) to help the client realize that he may feel free to seek the counselor's aid at anytime in the future.

Thus, counseling, as a time-oriented process, is differentiated from other human interactional processes by the five stages of directional movement. These stages are applicable regardless of the goals or expectancies of the client. Whether the goal is to help some person to reach an educational objective, some vocational decision, some understanding of his world, or some more general psychological help, the stages of the process are based on human needs and behavior and are, therefore, the same for all.

Index

Index

PRINTED IN U.S.A.